History of Argentina

A Captivating Guide to Argentine History, Starting from the Pre-Columbian Period Through the Inca Empire and Spanish Colonization to the Present

Free Bonus from Captivating History
(Available for a Limited time)

Hi History Lovers!

Now you have a chance to join our exclusive history list so you can get your first history ebook for free as well as discounts and a potential to get more history books for free! Simply visit the link below to join.

Captivatinghistory.com/ebook

Also, make sure to follow us on Facebook, Twitter and Youtube by searching for Captivating History.

Contents

INTRODUCTION 1

CHAPTER 1 – A LAND BEFORE HISTORY 2

CHAPTER 2 – INCA EMPIRE EXPANDS INTO ARGENTINA 7

CHAPTER 3 – TALL TALES AND ADVENTURES OF THE
EXPLORERS 11

CHAPTER 4 – THE BATTLE FOR BUENOS AIRES....................16

CHAPTER 5 – INDIGENOUS DECLINE AND THE CALCHAQUÍ
WARS..26

CHAPTER 6 – LA RECONQUISTA AND LA DEFENSA 32

CHAPTER 7 – THE PATH TOWARD INDEPENDENCE 39

CHAPTER 8 – THE MAY REVOLUTION.......................................42

CHAPTER 9 – THE WAR FOR INDEPENDENCE GAINS GROUND 56

CHAPTER 10 – "HANNIBAL OF THE ANDES" 62

CHAPTER 11 – A DECLARATION OF INDEPENDENCE 68

CHAPTER 12 – THE WARS WITHIN..71

CHAPTER 13 – THE ROSAS REGIME RISES................................74

CHAPTER 14 – RISE OF A REPUBLIC..80

CHAPTER 15 – A CONTROVERSIAL CAMPAIGN USHERS IN THE
"GOLDEN YEARS" 83

CHAPTER 16 – A CRISIS OF CULTURAL IDENTITY 87

CHAPTER 17 – WORKER STRIKES DESCEND INTO ANARCHY 92

CHAPTER 18 – THE GREAT DEPRESSION AND THE WORLD
AT WAR 99

CHAPTER 19 – THE PERÓN ERA BEGINS 104

CHAPTER 20 – THE RETURN OF PERÓN 109

CHAPTER 21 – THE "DIRTY WAR" AND THE FALKLAND WAR 113

CONCLUSION...116

HERE'S ANOTHER BOOK BY CAPTIVATING HISTORY THAT
YOU MIGHT LIKE...118

FREE BONUS FROM CAPTIVATING HISTORY (AVAILABLE
FOR A LIMITED TIME) 119

REFERENCES 120

Introduction

Argentina has a thrilling and complex history, from the natives' beautiful beginning to colonization by Spanish conquistadors, through the romance of rough-riding gauchos on the pampas to the heroic adventures of José de San Martín and the fight for independence, to the terror of repression instituted by various political and military regimes.

Named *Tierra Argentina* by Ruy Díaz de Guzmán in the early 1600s after the Latin word for silver—argentum—the world's eighth-largest country shines on its continent like the precious metal for which it is known. From the rugged magnificence of the Andes, the fertile grassy pampas (plains) teeming with animal and plant life, rocky plateaus, the famed Iguazu Falls—a place where nature brings together a combination of 270 separate waterfalls to create spectacular veils of white—to glacial Patagonia's "Land of Fire" (Tierra del Fuego) at the end of the continent, Argentina is certainly a land of epic beauty.

But the country has seen its share of struggles. It has been rightly said that Argentina's history has been written in blood. Its long history has seen many changes in cultures, leadership, and forms of government. Experience the country's soaring highs and crushing lows in this book.

Chapter 1 – A Land Before History

Though most people think of the origins of Argentina beginning with the Spanish conquistadors who landed on its shores, the reality is that there were indigenous people living there for thousands of years. There was a lot of diversity among the numerous tribes and cultural groups that lived here, though some tribes lived similar lifestyles based on what the land provided for them in their region.

Early tribes could be grouped into three basic kinds of lifestyles: those with basic hunting and gathering skills (living in Patagonia and the pampas), those who were highly skilled in using bows and arrows to hunt (like the Charrúa, Guaraní, and Minuane people), and basic farmers who were skilled with creating pottery.

Having made no written history, the people that lived here remain as one of history's mysteries. But not all was lost.

The first inhabitants, believed to be settlers in the Patagonia region, would gradually migrate a long way from their original lands. The ethnic origins of those who settled in Argentina were very diverse, but it appears highly likely that all originated from the tribes that crossed the Bering Strait into North America. From there, they would have traveled the length of two enormous continents—an especially long migration for those who made it to Patagonia, a strip of land tucked between the Pacific and Atlantic Oceans. The distance from any other civilization would have made this land feel like the end of the earth.

The first settlers who walked into Patagonia would have stared in awe at a dramatic and sweeping landscape cut by glaciers and lava. Bright blue and brilliant white glacial ice would have spilled out through the high mountain passes, a strikingly beautiful type of desolation among the jagged peaks of ice and stone. Those who came to the land now known as Argentina followed the long mountainous spine of the Andes and eventually made their way to the Atlantic Ocean, where the dizzying mountain heights would fade into rugged, windswept sea cliffs.

The relatively cooler desert temperatures and dry air in the region would have been a relief for the people who had migrated through the humid heat of the northern tropical areas. However, the people who traveled to the coastal region found that, despite the nutrient-rich soil in the ground, there was very little soil water for the plants to utilize. Then there was the problem of the weather, which would make for an almost non-existent growing season. The people would have found some hardy scrub brush and grasses, along with a few courageous pine and beech tree varieties that were determined to survive their relatively inhospitable environment.

Being in such isolated areas meant they couldn't rely on any other peoples to survive—they were even essentially cut off from the larger civilizations in the Central Andes. They were on their own in this new and isolated land, so they had to become self-sufficient. They would have to turn to the land and the sea to provide for them.

The Yamanas people, who made their homes on the coasts and islands of Tierra del Fuego, became skilled at surviving off of the ocean. They used the bark of the relatively few trees that grew in the land to make canoes for traveling and catching fish, crabs, and mollusks for food. It was not just the men who did this work, as it was necessary for the whole family to work for their food. Women showed their strength in rowing the canoes through the chilly waters of the narrow fjords. The men knelt or stood at the edge of the boat and scanned the waters for food, harpoon in hand, ready for a quick strike. The children did their part as well, tending the warming fires built into the soil and stones at the base of the canoe.

A family would bring their day's catch back home to their branch huts, a home with a dug-out center that made the living space partially underground. The dug-out earth would keep them cool in the dry heat, and in colder temperatures, the family would warm themselves by wearing soft, silky, and waterproof otter and seal skins.

The indigenous people who stayed in the interior areas away from the coast lived in a land blessed with abundance.[1] They lived in lush green valleys and pastoral plains dotted with life-giving rivers and lakes, surrounded by plentiful animal and plant life. They lived in a land among countless free-roaming guanacos, swift-footed rheas, and wandering horse herds.[2]

Some people lived an agricultural life, while others hunted guanacos and other animals for food. Those in the northeast tamed the wild horses to become skilled riders. Besides having a close relationship with the land, the crude pottery and paintings they left as part of their legacy show that the indigenous people were creative and artistic.

Though some indigenous people, like the Tehuelche in Patagonia and the Querandí and Puelche living on the pampas, remained nomadic hunters and fishers,[3] others like the Diaguita and Guaraní

---

[1] The indigenous tribe who lived in the interior were called the Ona or Selk'nam, members of the Tehuelche people. The coastal Yamanas were also descended from the Tehuelche, making them related peoples.

[2] Guanacos are four-legged animals closely related to llamas and alpacas, though relatively smaller in stature. The Ona were skilled at hunting guanacos, and in later years, this became a large part of their economy. Rheas are related to ostriches.

[3] Pampas are fertile grasslands with abundant wildlife.

people eventually evolved their relatively wild existences into a more settled lifestyle.[4] They created permanent cities, settlements, and small villages and lived an agricultural life, cultivating maize, yucca, sweet potatoes, and even honey.[5] Within these settlements, people lived a communal life with no real thought to private or personal property. In fact, the people of some tribes shared communal homes with up to ten or fifteen families living in the same structure.

Life progressed from these simple settlements as people began to build impressive and monumental architectures, create tools and other metal works from silver and copper, and form complex societies with hierarchies. Though most tribes did not have chiefs, they were led by local shamans—wise men and prophets who enjoyed an elite and important status in the communities. They were connected with the supernatural and sorcery, causing the people to fear death by the dark arts.

There were no structured religions, but as noted, the people did lean toward the spiritual. Because of their heavy reliance on the earth, it is little wonder that their worship was largely nature-based.

Though little is known about their beliefs, a prime example of this nature worship was found with the early Guaraní people, who believed that divinity was all around them, particularly within all living things.[6] The development of their mythology included a pantheon of gods, as well as legendary animist characters such as werewolves, glowworms, and a giant lily (based on the legend of Irupé, a woman who fell in love with the moon).

---

[4] Guaraní was a name given by the Spanish and possibly translated to "warrior,"

[5] Some tribes built subterranean houses halfway into the hillsides.

[6] This form of worship is closely associated with animistic pantheism, a belief that all living beings are connected through the same spiritual essence, giving people, animals, plants, and even minerals the ability to have a sort of living reincarnation.

However, various tribes had their own mythologies, and although the characters were similar in nature, they were known by different names (similar to the correlation between ancient Roman and Greek mythological figures).

They also had their own rites of passage, such as the coming-of-age Hain ritual for Selk'nam males. During this rite, boys were taken to a fear-inspiring dark hut where they were to unmask the "spirits" that they had been taught to fear while growing up. Summoning up their courage, they unmasked what was lurking in the darkness, finding that these "spirits" were actually humans in disguise. Their bravery was rewarded with a telling of their people's beliefs about the creation of the world, the sun, and the moon.

Body paint, an important cultural and creative expression, was used throughout many of the Argentine cultures. Among the Selk'nam, body paint wasn't just ornamental but also had symbolic and social significance. They painted over almost any exposed body surface, including the face. Individuals put their own unique touch on their personal paint, which served as something of an identity. But paint was also used in rituals, such as the Hain ritual, as well as to signify social statuses and roles like shaman, changes in status like a girl becoming a woman, or to act as camouflage.

It is also notable that a later Jesuit missionary, Martin Dobrizhoffer, remarked that some of the tribal people practiced cannibalism, likely as part of funeral rituals, after which the dead were placed in large jars and buried upside down in the ground.

While the smaller cultures in the south were developing, so was the mighty Inca Empire of Andean Peru. The mighty nation was expanding and absorbing peoples and cultures in all directions, and by the early 15th century, it had set its sights on the Argentinian tribes. But not all the tribes were about to be conquered without a fight.

Chapter 2 – Inca Empire Expands into Argentina

As the mighty Inca Empire expanded its reach through South America, the Inca made their way to the northwest region of Argentina around 1450 CE. Rather than having tactical genius, the Incas conquered based on the size and excellent organization of their army. Boys as young as ten years old from villages around the empire were trained and drafted into the military service. So, when the Inca army of emperor Topa Inca Yupanqui moved swiftly along the vast road system they had built and entered the Argentinian lands, they came in droves.

It's possible that the Incas were attracted to the precious mineral and metal resources of the land. The chance to have unlimited access to silver, zinc, and copper was a temptation too difficult to resist.

As they appeared on the plains of the Tafí Valley, swept through the rusted rainbow-colored peaks of Cerro de los Siete Colores, and invaded the narrow mountain valley of Quebrada de Humahuaca, the nearly 200,000 warriors must have appeared to be an invincible force. Again, they used sheer size as part of their strategy, hoping to intimidate villages and settlements into surrendering and only fighting when necessary.

In fact, when the Inca came into settlements and villages in the northwest region, they employed a peaceful strategy of trying to establish good relationships with tribal heads. When coming upon a settlement, the Inca presented the chief with gifts of wool clothing, mullu (a type of oyster thought to be food for the gods), and coca leaves. If the chief accepted the gifts, it meant that the people accepted Inca authority. The only other option was a bloody war. There was a difficult choice to be made.

For the most part, the Incas did not have to fight. When the Inca soldiers came dressed in their quilted tunics and shields of the province from which they hailed, and when their military commanders appeared with wooden or wild animal skin helmets gleaming with precious stones and the plumes of tropical feathers rising from their heads, people took notice. When highly skilled warriors with slings, bows, copper or boned-tipped arrows, lances, short swords, and battle-axes appeared in the land, there was little question about what would happen should they resist. Most areas simply did not have the manpower to fight them. The people knew that refusal to acquiesce would almost surely lead to death and defeat. Therefore, most accepted that they had no other option than to come under Inca rule.

Though it may have been the better option for the majority, the Inca rule would change their lives drastically, at least for the most part. Society as they knew it would also be different. Many of the conquered would be resettled in different areas, some possibly even being transported to serve as laborers in Chilean mines. Being shifted around and resettled in different areas among different peoples and being introduced to new traditions and ways would mean a change in their culture and a dramatic shift in what they had known all their lives. Their whole identities would begin to take on a new shape.

Local chiefs were replaced by rulers who followed the Inca administrative model, making for a more standardized form of government across conquered lands. These new rulers were men loyal to the Inca emperor. Some of these new rulers were children who had been taken from conquered peoples and brought to the impressive city capital of Cusco. There, they grew up being educated by the Incas, married to women within the Inca nobility, and then returned to their native land. This way, the Incas could establish ties with the indigenous conquered peoples through marriage alliances.

With the mighty empire standing behind them, these new rulers had more power than the local chiefs ever had. The people had to learn to live with a new set of laws and a societal structure that was different from their own. Inca law was strictly and often harshly administered. Not surprisingly, murder and theft were punishable crimes, but even seemingly minor offenses, such as laziness, were subject to the harshest penalty. First-time offenders got off relatively easy with "just" the humiliation of a public scolding. But those who broke the law a second time would face a brutal death by hanging, being pushed over a cliff, or stoning.

Inca colonization had its benefits as well. New architectural structures were introduced as they built administrative and military buildings, as well as storehouses. Native tribes were introduced to important and, in their eyes, more advanced infrastructure like road systems, bridges, tunnels, and irrigation systems.

More sophisticated economies were also introduced. The empire demanded an annual tax (called a mit'a) from the conquered people, but since there was no currency, payment had to be made another way. Mit'a was sometimes paid using cattle, crops, or textiles, but the preferred method of payment was work. That meant two- or three-month-long services as a soldier, messenger, road builder, farmer, or any other kind of worker that was needed. Those that paid the tax through work could not tend their lands during that time. This created a hardship for those who needed to care for crops or livestock and resulted in some loss. It meant they were forced to sacrifice some of their prosperity in the name of working for the empire. But this system also enabled the Inca government to create early forms of social programs to provide clothing, food, and medicines for those who needed them.

The Calchaquí Diaguita people, however, would not accept this fate. They knew that even peaceful conquest meant that their leaders would be executed and replaced by Inca representatives and that their culture would be assimilated and perhaps completely lost.

Their very name and the region they lived in, known as the Calchaquí Valley, is literally translated "where the Inca empire ends."[7] And that it truly was, as the southernmost boundary of the Inca territory stopped at their valley.

With their record of conquest, the Inca likely thought the Calchaquí would be easy to overtake.

However, the warlike Calchaquí built strategic stone fortifications throughout their territory as a defense and were skilled in battle. When the Inca armies tried to enter the Argentinian Calchaquí territory from Bolivia, there was an unpleasant surprise waiting for them. They likely did not expect the Calchaquís' fierce resistance and were pushed back in defeat.

Though the Inca, the Calchaquí, and the rest of the indigenous Argentinians did not yet know it, there was a more formidable enemy sailing toward their shores—one that was a threat to them all. The fierce warrior legacy of the Calchaquí, in particular, would serve them well in the years to come as they fought off colonization by another advanced civilization—European colonizers.

---

[7] However, some sources contest that the name was derived from the Spaniards and meant "very courageous."

Chapter 3 – Tall Tales and Adventures of the Explorers

As the people along the shoreline of Martín García Island in the Río de la Plata went about their daily lives in February 1516, they looked up to see three wooden boats, Spanish caravels, coming up the river. Although they were small boats by European standards, they were massive compared to the canoes the indigenous people used. Staring curiously, they watched as the boats carrying seventy men neared their shoreline.

On the lead caravel, Pilot-Major Juan Díaz de Solís spotted simple huts dotting the river's coast. His crew pointed out that there was a number of native people standing at the shoreline, signaling them to come ashore. Wanting to capture some of the people to take back to Spain, de Solís stopped the ship and leaped ashore with only a sword in hand. Several crew members and officers followed him, equally eager to capture human souvenirs. They were wholly ill-prepared for what happened next.

Suddenly, a shower of arrows rained down upon the Spaniards. As they turned to run, a second volley of arrows struck their targets and laid the men to the ground. The Guaraní put an end to those who had not died immediately and stripped the bodies of what they could take.

All but one, a cabin boy (*grumete*) named Francisco del Puerto, were killed in front of the crew who remained on the ships. As the rest of the explorers looked on from the relative safety of their ships, they watched the Guaraní as they dismembered their crewmates before their eyes and built a great fire whereupon they roasted their kill and ate the bodies.[8]

Overcome with horror, the rest of the expedition scrambled to leave, de Solís's brother-in-law Francisco de Torres, taking charge of the expedition. Poor young del Puerto ran from the attack, but his shipmates were unable to rescue him, so he was left behind with the indigenous people who had just killed his captain and crewmates.[9]

Although some sources credit Juan Díaz de Solís as the first European to land in Argentina, documentation by Amerigo Vespucci suggests that he was the first to discover the Río de la Plata and that he had even sailed as far as Tierra del Fuego in Patagonia. Fourteen years before de Solís set foot on the banks of the Río de la Plata, his Pilot-Major predecessor Vespucci had extensively explored the coast of South America, including Argentina.

Whether de Solís had truly been the first or whether Vespucci had beaten him to it, neither explorer would be the last to land on Argentina's shores.

In 1520, Ferdinand Magellan retraced de Solís's route along the coast and made his way to Argentina's southern shores. The expedition stopped in Patagonia, and when Magellan and his men met

---

[8] Though it has classically been stated that the Charrúa people killed de Solís and his men, further studies have found this to be unlikely since they did not practice cannibalism. The Guaraní people, however, did practice cannibalism, so modern historians lean toward naming that tribe as the one that killed de Solís.

[9] Some sources cite his name as Francisco Marquina. He was stranded along the Río de la Plata for ten years before finally being rescued in 1526 by an expedition led by Sebastian Cabot. On being found by Cabot, he related terrible stories of being a slave for the Guaraní people since his capture.

the indigenous people living in the area, there was something about them that caught the explorers by surprise.

The first thing that struck them was the people's unusually large feet. The immense size of their sandals appeared to be like snowshoes to the visitors. Magellan also noticed something cleverly practical about the natives' footwear—they stuffed tufts of grass into their shoes in order to keep their feet warm. The Spanish explorers on the expedition called the people *patagones*, meaning "big feet."

The size of the people gave way to exaggerated tales, starting with Magellan's official expedition chronicler, Italian Antonio Pigafetta. According to Pigafetta, when their ship came close to the shore, they spotted a strange and colossal figure "singing and dancing on the sand." Curious, Magellan sent some of the crew ashore to take a better look. When they came back, Pigafetta recorded their shocking report. "This man was so tall that our heads hardly came up to his belt. He was well formed; his face was broad and colored with red, excepting that his eyes were surrounded with yellow." He estimated that the man he saw was eight feet tall. The long mantles, tall, muscular forms, and, by some accounts, athletic prowess of the Patagonians surely fed into the myth of the Patagonian giants.[10]

As word of the giants spread around Europe, other explorers had their curiosity piqued. These included Sir Francis Drake, who, after finding the Patagonian people himself, reported them to be seven feet, six inches tall.[11] Over the next few hundred years, numerous other

---

[10] One chronicler claimed that besides ball games and running, a couple of Patagonians walked forty to fifty miles to a trading station over a fourteen-hour period, having no food and appearing to have no ill effects or distress upon reaching the station.

[11] For nearly three hundred years, this topic fascinated Europe. In 1764, Commodore John "Foul-Weather Jack" Byron, grandfather to famed poet Lord Byron, took a circumnavigation expedition in large part to find out more information on the Patagonian people. Though initially not specifying any height, he called them "people who in size come the nearest to giants of any people I believe in the world." Not long after his return to London, two publications quoted him as saying the people were eight feet, six inches tall.

explorers would make similar dubious claims, possibly influenced by the incredible rumors sweeping Europe.

Other explorers came to Argentina with the hope of finding enormous stores of treasures. Sebastian Cabot was drawn to further explore the river that was then known as the Mar Dulce. He had been encouraged by stories of riches as told by the rescued Francisco del Puerto. Expecting to find vast stores of silver and other precious metals, he renamed the Mar Dulce the Río de la Plata (the same river de Solís and his men took on their ill-fated journey).

Some of the native people Cabot encountered wore plates of gold in their noses and ears, which, to Cabot, was a good sign that they had access to treasures. In his dealings with the locals, he was able to exchange some items for gold and silver trinkets, and he was also told that he could find mountains of gold upriver. The journey, however, did not produce the windfall he had expected. Still, Cabot was convinced that abundant treasures existed in this land, and undeterred, he returned to Spain in hopes of convincing the crown to fund return trips to find the wealth that he was sure was there.

Some explorers were compelled to search for the legendary City of the Caesars (also known at times as the Wandering City, Trapananda or Trapalanda, Lin Lin, and the City of Patagonia). The stories of the mythological city came to life during a 1529 expedition led by Captain Francisco César. During their month-and-a-half-long march west and return trip to their ships, he and his men likely came across native peoples who told them tales of vast wealth within the Inca Empire (mainly Peru), including gems, gold, and silver. Though the Incas did have access to or owned valuable items made from these precious materials, the fanciful stories of Inca wealth were spun over and over again until they took on mythological proportions.

Described as sitting between two unknown Andean mountains, one alleged to be made of gold and the other of diamonds, the City of the Caesars was said to be a civilization shimmering with an enormous wealth of gold, silver, and diamonds. As the legend of the city took on mystical characteristics, some claimed that it was enchanted and only appeared at certain times. Others claimed it was built by shipwreck survivors or more eerily founded by ghosts. But the reward for those who found it was always the same—a vast fortune in shiny treasures. It was that treasure that drove explorers, including Jesuit friars, mad with treasure fever as they searched the Andes for a storehouse of wealth that did not exist.

Stories of treasures led to competition among explorers and various sponsoring countries, and in turn, the fight to establish settlements led to aggression between the Europeans and natives. Friendly trade and curiosity gave way to conquistadors and colonization.

Chapter 4 – The Battle for Buenos Aires

The Spaniards who first came to Argentina may have envisioned seeing advanced civilizations like those found in the Peruvian Inca territory (cities such as Cusco or Machu Pichu) or in the Meso-American region (Mexico and Central America). However, great cities with advanced cultures and impressive step pyramids were nowhere to be found. Instead, they found a country that, outside of the northwest area, was sparsely populated by a variety of disparate cultures.

These simple stone houses, "cities" with populations of no more than three thousand, ceremonial buildings, and the people's agricultural lifestyle might have been underwhelming. Despite their simple lifestyle, the Spanish adventurers' journals said that they found the people they met to be intelligent and valiant.

At first, settlements were relatively easy to establish. These settlements were no more advanced than those of the native tribes living there. Some shipwrecked Spaniards even coexisted in native settlements. Before treasure-hunter Sebastian Cabot returned to Europe, he established the first European settlement in Argentina near what is now known as Rosario.

Motivated by competition with Portugal for conquest, Spain's goal was to halt Portuguese expansion by way of Brazil. Bolstered by their victory over Peru, Spain began a series of repeated attempts to colonize Argentina. Those attempts and successes began to reshape Argentina into the country we know today.

One of the most well-known settlements came into being due to Pedro de Mendoza, a Spanish nobleman, soldier, and explorer. After a journey fraught with lost ships, rivalries between sub-commanders, the execution of a mutinous officer, and Mendoza's own bout of illness with syphilis (which rendered him ineffective as a commander), the expedition finally arrived at the Río de la Plata in early 1536.

It was there that the Spanish expedition encountered the nearly three thousand nomadic Querandí people living throughout the region. The people treated the Spanish hospitably. Though food was scarce even for them, the Querandí shared what little fish and meat they had with the newcomers.

For fourteen days, the people shared their meager provisions with the Spanish, but on the fifteenth day, the Querandí were nowhere to be found. During the night, the Querandí had picked up their settlement and moved several miles away. Having come to rely on the Querandís' provisions and even more so having come to take it for granted, the Spaniards were somewhat put out by the abrupt move.

Mendoza sent some deputies to the new Querandí encampment to find out what went wrong. Though the deputies made promises and proposed various plans to continue receiving food supplies, the Querandí no longer wanted to deal with the Spanish. Angry and exasperated, the deputies began to make threats against the people, promising punishment if they did not get what they wanted. Though there may have been a language barrier between the Spanish and the Querandí, the intent of the threat was clear.

The Querandí did not take kindly to the hostility and pounced upon the three emissaries, beating them before sending them fleeing back to their own encampment. Incensed, Mendoza sent his brother at the command of three hundred soldiers and thirty horsemen to retaliate against the Querandí. Mendoza thought he would teach the Querandí a lesson and show who was the superior force, but he was sorely mistaken.

With their horses weak and malnourished and the Querandí waiting for them in battle position, the Spanish were at a disadvantage before the battle even began. When the Spanish crossed a small river of water (later named the Luján River), the Querandí were ready for them. The sound of a furious thundering charge broke out as the Querandí rushed upon the Spanish, driving them back to the slippery riverbanks. Unable to gain a good footing, the Spanish were met with an unrelenting barrage of arrows, lances, and stones flung from bola slings.

The Querandí chased the Spanish back across the stream, where the battle continued, both sides taking heavy losses. Mendoza's brother was one of the thirty Spanish who lay dead on the battlefield. After losing hundreds of their own warriors, the Querandí were driven off, and the weakened Spanish force returned to their own camp but not before taking some of the weapons and provisions that the natives had left behind.

The Spanish began to build up their settlement, erecting a protective three-foot-thick adobe mud wall around their new "city," with a stronger fortress built at one end. Because the wall had been made hastily without giving the mud proper time to dry in the sun, every rainstorm eroded the wall, and their protective barrier began to actually melt away.

Though the Spaniards' battle with the Querandí was considered a victory, and they were now somewhat protected by a fortress and a wall, the Spanish were about to face a foe that was far worse than the native warriors—famine.

As food became scarce, desperation began to set in. The colonists began to catch rodents, lizards, and snakes to eat. As the famine started to become even more desperate, they resorted to eating any available leather rawhides, including their shoes. Then came the unthinkable. The famine had become so hopeless that some began to eat the bodies of those who had died—the very cannibalistic acts that they called the natives barbarians for.

The Spaniards' problems with famine did not halt the hostilities that had grown between them and the surrounding native peoples. The natives formed a coalition and attacked the Spanish city numerous times. One of Mendoza's soldiers later reported that about 23,000 native tribesmen came upon the city in one of the attacks. Using arrows tipped with straw, they would ignite the tinder and let the burning projectiles fly over the mud wall, consuming the buildings inside with flames. While the bowmen shot fire, others attacked the settlers with weapons in hand. The city as much as burnt to the ground several times, with the Spanish barely making it out alive.

As all this was occurring, Mendoza's syphilis worsened, and he suffered almost constantly. Between his health and the disappointment he felt over the constant attacks, he knew he was going to have to leave the city he founded. Finally, in 1537, he set sail to return to Spain. Still, he did not leave his city unattended. He left a force behind and promised to send help and supplies. He would never reach Spain. Mendoza died on the long journey, and his body was sent overboard into the deep sea. He would never again see the Argentinian city he helped start, Santa María del Buen Ayre (later known as Buenos Aires). He did, however, beg in his final will that the people left behind be sent all necessary provisions and aid.

Although Mendoza appointed Juan de Ayolas as his successor before he left, the city floundered from persistent attacks and lack of necessities. The survivors could no longer stay, especially since they had found none of the grand wealth they had anticipated. They fled to the more strongly fortified city of Asunción, previously founded by Ayolas after a treaty with the Guaraní.

While Santa María del Buen Ayre lay abandoned, Jerónimo Luis de Cabrera was ignoring his orders from the viceroy of Peru and the Spanish crown. Recently having been made governor of Tucumán, he was ordered to build a fort in the province now known as Santiago del Estero with the goal of colonizing the area. The Salta Valley would be a strategic colony for trade and communication between Tucumán and Charcas. Cabrera decided he would rather make his mark farther south.

Enticed by stories of "cities of gold," his quest south was two-fold. He would look for the City of the Caesars, as well as found a province that had access to the Atlantic Ocean. Taking one hundred soldiers and forty wagons laden with supplies, he set out on a route along the Estero River, his travels taking him into the territory of the Comechingón and Sanavirón tribes. On June 24th, 1573, the expedition set up their first settlement. Within days, it collapsed. The colonists looked for a more suitable location and found one on the shores of the Suquía River.

On July 6th, 1573, perhaps with the winter morning chill still in the air, numbing the hands and feet of the soldiers, Cabrera came to a place he thought would be good for raising cattle—a necessity for those pioneering new territory. There, his expedition stopped to survey the beautiful VALLEY THAT SURROUNDED THEM. Making his decision, Cabrera drew his sword and announced that a new city had been brought to birth. Cabrera and the settlers built a fort in the first city of his southern advancement. In honor of his late wife's native province in Spain,[12,13] he named it Córdoba de la Nueva Andalucía (later known simply as Córdoba).[14]

---

[12] Tragically, Cabrera's wife, Catalina Dorantes de Trejo, had died in a 1555 shipwreck, along with two of their children.

Cabrera, for his part, would not stay in Córdoba but continued moving west in his explorations, looking for a good place to establish a port that would connect Tucumán with the Atlantic Ocean. As he traveled down the Paraná River, he eventually met up with Juan de Garay, who had just established the city of Santa Fe in that area. Garay was also looking for a route connecting to the ocean, and an argument ensued. Neither of the men actually had permission for that quest, but it didn't stop them from arguing over who had the real rights to it. The matter was resolved only when Cabrera was called back to Córdoba to help pacify the Comechingón, who were about to attack the city. He didn't realize that a different enemy would meet him there.

Gonzalo de Abreu had already made quite an entrance when he arrived at the city of Santiago del Estero. He brought a military apparatus to its borders and entered the city by means of war. The city cabildo (city council) did not take kindly to this unnecessary show of force, and when Abreu immediately went to them upon entering the city, they understandably met him with violence. The people of the city were annoyed by the aggression of Abreu and his delegation as well. One colonist, Martín Moreno, went up to Abreu and asked, "Friend, entering your own house do you enter this way? Are we traitors here? Or are you?" It was a just foreshadow of how Abreu's tyrannical rule over the province would operate.

Upon finding his predecessor Cabrera was away, Abreu took stock of his possessions, finding that he had many valuable assets in the city. Although illegal, the first thing he did was seize everything owned by Cabrera. Knowing that Cabrera had disobeyed the orders of the viceroy and went on expeditions of his own accord, Abreu wanted to

---

[13] Cabrera may have also thought the name was fitting due to the Comechingón tribe's physical resemblance to the Spanish Andalusians.

[14] The location of Córdoba was moved from its original spot by Gómez Suárez de Figueroa just four years after its establishment. Córdoba, according to Cabrera's plan, was to be the seat of government in his newly formed Nueva Andalucía province.

capitalize on what he saw as an opportunity. He sent two men to Córdoba ahead of him, armed with Cabrera's official dismissal. Three days later, he himself left Santiago del Estero and went to Córdoba, intent on hunting Cabrera down.

When Abreu entered Córdoba, an ailing and weak Cabrera left his sickbed to meet him. He accorded Abreu the honors of his position as governor, despite having felt disillusioned and unappreciated by his dismissal. Abreu, on the other hand, extended no such courtesies. Cabrera's banner was snatched from the hands of his son, dragging him to the ground. Abreu immediately ordered Cabrera's arrest, and after chaining him like a criminal, he had him sent back to Santiago del Estero.

Abreu made sure that Cabrera endured weeks of abhorrent torture while imprisoned in the city. Then came his "trial," a sinister mockery of justice that bore no resemblance to a legal proceeding. Cabrera was accused of conspiring and mutiny against the representatives of the Spanish crown for not having settled the Salta Valley as he had been ordered by the viceroy. Abreu's intent was clear: he wanted to get rid of Cabrera permanently. The sham trial ended with Cabrera being sentenced to death. Because he was a hidalgo (a Spanish gentleman), the execution could not be done by garroting (strangulation with a rope or chain). Instead, he was afforded a noble's death by beheading, a punishment that was carried out on August 17th, 1574.

Cabrera's body was wrapped in animal skins, preserved with salts, and buried by the Suquía River until his remains could be taken back to Spain. Before he could be returned to his homeland, however, a flood came, washing his body away, never to be found.

Juan de Garay, for his part, narrowly escaped Abreu's reach. In 1576, Abreu ordered Garay's arrest and had him taken to Santiago del Estero, where his one-time rival had been executed just two years earlier. The thought must have chilled Garay to his bones.

Garay, however, was fortunate enough to be released. He used that freedom to return to Santa Fe, and from there, he formed his own expedition to find the cities of gold. Taking a group of more than forty men and women, he traveled down the Carcarañá River to a place near the abandoned Sancti Spiritu fort. Entering a lagoon, the group decided to camp on the banks of the river for the night. They were not alone. The native Querandí in the area saw their arrival, and during the night, they ambushed the expedition. Garay was one of the fifteen killed in the attack, which took place in 1583.

Before his death, however, he would revive the ruins of Santa María del Buen Ayre. Though she had lain desolate for decades, Garay made sure that it that would not be the end for Buenos Ares. As acting governor of Asunción and captain-general of the Río de la Plata region, Garay would bring the city to life again. Three years before his death, he took sixty families and returned to Buenos Aires to rebuild her from the ruins. But the re-settlers did not go without incentive. Not able to promise the wealth in the form of silver or gold, Garay enticed the settlers to follow him back to Buenos Aires with the promise of something else of high value—horses.

After splitting into three groups, Garay sailed his contingent from Asunción, followed on land by a group led by his nephew, known by the less-than-inspiring nickname "dog face."[15] Garay's group included a woman named Ana Díaz.[16] Though initially, Garay had made a "no women" rule for this first phase of the expedition, Díaz fought to be part of the first group to prepare Buenos Aires for re-settlement. She believed it was her calling to go, and Garay relented.

---

[15] His real name was Alonso de Vera.

[16] Although historical records of Ana Díaz have been somewhat obscured, some sources label her as a prostitute who followed the men from Asunción while others hail her as a rare female conquistador.

The first re-settlers made it to the remains of old Santa María del Buen Ayre on May 28th, 1580. Two weeks later, Garay and his men were set up for the reestablishment of the city, which they would now call Ciudad de Trinidad (City of the Trinity). Families were now able to come and buy properties and settle. Among those who bought property lots was Ana Díaz, the first woman to own property in the city.

It wasn't only Europeans who came to the newly rebuilt city. The initial population of the city came to include two hundred Guaraní, mainly families. The settlers and native people would now coexist peacefully within the city.

Far from the more "Wild West" type structure of its predecessor, the new city was founded on laws and religious requirements as set out by their majesty back in Spain, King Philip II.

The founding act was signed by Garay, making the reestablishment official in the eyes of the Spanish law and crown. After the signing, Garay took his official oath in front of the authorities and had a Catholic cross planted in the midst of the city. Putting up this religious symbol was nothing unusual, but it was what Garay did next that was curious. He commanded that "a stick or wood be raised by public roll." This emblematic stick, symbolic of the carob tree, was a visual reminder to the settlers that the laws of the city would be strictly enforced and that crime would not be tolerated.[17] Those who defied the law would be tied to a carob tree and executed. The stick was to remain where it was planted, and any who dared destroy or remove it would be subject to the harshest penalty—an immediate death.

Despite the stricter laws that now held order in the city, the re-settlers received benefits for their troubles. They were given large tracts of land where the previously abandoned pastoral animals had thrived and multiplied. The promised horses, on the other hand, were

---

[17] The carob tree was, at that time, a symbol of justice.

nowhere to be had. The expansive flat stretches of land made them difficult to catch, and even if they did, there was no room in the city for all the corrals.

It would not be the end to the settlers' troubles. They faced the back-breaking tasks of rebuilding and replanting as the assaults by the native tribes continued to plague them. The city, somewhat relegated to a backwater town in comparison with more important cities like Santiago del Estero and Córdoba, would continue its modest growth.[18] It was established as a permanent colonial city and an important strategic location for defending the southern half of the Spanish territory from Portuguese conquistadors. However, the fight between the native tribes and the Spanish was far from over.

---

[18] Córdoba remained one of the most important cities of colonial Argentina. It gained a strong Jesuit presence by the early 1600s, and the religious order established the first university in Argentina (the Universidad Nacional de Córdoba) in 1613. It is one of the oldest universities in South America. To this day, Córdoba is still the country's most important educational center.

Chapter 5 – Indigenous Decline and the Calchaquí Wars

The indigenous peoples of Argentina carried out a long campaign of resistance against the Spanish conquistadors and colonizers. Yet, their numbers began to wane as the 17th century began. Having a population of about 105,000 before the Spanish landed, their numbers were ravaged due to several factors, including the tiniest of conquerors.

Unbeknownst to the indigenous tribes, the Spanish had brought something far more deadly than their swords and machines of war—they brought disease. Though diseases like smallpox, influenza, typhus, and pneumonic plagues were more common (and survivable) among Europeans, they introduced exotic biological invaders to the natives. Since they had never been exposed to them before, their immune systems were unequipped for defense.

Despite military successes against Spain, the indigenous tribes still took heavy losses of life. Even though the native people had the home-field advantage due to their intricate knowledge of the land, firepower and horses won out. The Spanish proved to have the superior advantage on the battlefield.

Some of those healthy tribespeople that survived disease and war faced a fate that was perhaps even worse. As colonies grew, so did their need for labor. Help was needed for growing crops and caring for livestock, so what help the Spanish needed they took in the form of indigenous slaves. And when the mining trade opened up, the need for labor increased there too. Again, the colonists turned to forced labor to aid in their operations. This harsh life further reduced the indigenous population numbers.

These things also took a toll on their family structure and communities. As family members and relatives died in wars and massacres or were taken as slaves, communities began to shatter and fall apart. The population further suffered as increasing numbers of native women stopped having children—they could not bear to bring offspring into that turbulent world. Many who had children did the unthinkable, killing their babies as they were born. They considered it a kindness to save their child from a life of disease, famine, and slavery. These losses, coupled with their rapidly disappearing culture, took a harsh mental and emotional toll on adults in the indigenous communities. Some became so distraught that they believed they could no longer live in that world, committing suicide to end their suffering.

But many found ways to survive this new world. As long as they had breath and life in their bodies, some would continue to take every opportunity to resist and free themselves from the Spanish yoke that had come upon them. Even if that opportunity came with a dubious distinction.

From the mid-1500s to the mid-1600s, the Calchaquí tribes rebelled against the forced labor and tribute demands of the encomienda system laid upon them by the Spanish settlements. In trying to subdue native resistance, Spanish Captain Julián Cedeño believed that they might listen to one of their own. Cedeño captured a man named Chumbicha and turned him over to Governor Juan Pérez de Zurita, the founder of Córdoba de Calchaquí. They forced

Chumbicha into negotiations with his brother, an Inca magistrate (curaca or kuraka) of the town of Tolombón. Chumbicha's brother naively accepted the terms of negotiation, including having a Christian baptism. From then on, he was known as Juan Calchaquí.

It was not long before Juan Calchaquí's eyes were figuratively opened to the deal he had made with the Spanish. Zurita's lieutenant, Gregorio de Castañeda, mistreated the former curaca, which led to poor relations. Then Calchaquí began to realize the unfair and unequal treatment his people would be subject to under the encomienda. No longer willing to comply, his reaction was one of violence. He summoned warriors from surrounding indigenous communities and led them in a fierce uprising, attacking three Spanish cities that had been founded by Zurita. The native coalition drove out the colonists of all three cities, and as the people fled to nearby settlements, the natives chased them down and killed everyone they caught up to—men, women, and children. Few survived to make it to a safe location. While some chased after the fleeing Spanish, others stayed behind and razed the cities to the ground.

Spurred on by the Calchaquís' success, the Omaguaca people revolted shortly afterward, destroying Ciudad de Nieva (San Salvador de Jujuy). These attacks forced most of the colonists in the Tucumán province into the city of Santiago del Estero. The First Calchaquí War would be a major setback for the conquistadors and Spain. It came to be seen by the Spanish as one of the greatest tragedies in their history. But it would be just the first in a series of wars and rebellions with the native confederations, with conflicts such as the Viltipoco Rebellion and the Second Calchaquí War breaking out.

But in 1656, a man with a brownish complexion approached the native Calchaquí people of the Diaguita confederation. His young indigenous wife alongside him, he spoke to them in fluent Quechua. To their surprise, he told them his name—Inca Hualpa, the last descendant of the Inca emperors. He had arrived to help them fight off the Spanish. The Calchaquí may have had their doubts about this story, and they didn't like the idea of Inca subjugation, but the chance to oppose the Spanish presence more forcefully was hard to pass up.[19] Inca Hualpa assured the Calchaquí that as subjects under his Inca rule, he would do everything he could to help them drive the Spanish from the land—all they had to do was reveal the location of the rumored hidden Inca treasures.

In reality, Inca Hualpa was Pedro Bohórquez, a Spanish adventurer with schemes of finding South American treasure hoards. He had heard a vague rumor that the Calchaquí people knew of a secret location loaded with hidden Inca Empire gold and silver. He hatched the Inca Hualpa scheme to increase his odds of finding it.

At the same time as he was making promises to the Calchaquí, he was making equally unreliable promises to the Spanish. He told them about how he had convinced the native people that he was their rightful Inca emperor and, therefore, could get the people to not only submit to the Spanish crown but also tell them the location of the hidden treasure. All the Spanish had to do in return was guarantee him a position as a local leader. Capitalizing on the Jesuits' failure to convert the Calchaquí, he also assured them that as a Christian ruler, he would be able to get his people to convert to Christianity. The Spanish eagerly took the bait.

In June of 1657, Bohórquez entered the city of Póman in spectacular fashion. He arrived with all the pomp expected of an emperor, regally attired in Inca clothing and escorted by a number of curacas. The Spanish received him with all the honors and respect due to such a high personage.

The Catholic bishop of the province, Melchor de Maldonado y Saavedra, was highly suspicious of Bohórquez and his incredible story. The incredulous bishop and several other officials openly opposed the appointment but were unable to convince the governor.

---

[19] The Calchaquí did not only resist the colonizing attempts by the Spanish but also the evangelical attempts of the Jesuits to convert them to Christianity.

The governor of Tucumán, Alonso Mercado y Villacorta, bestowed upon Bohórquez the title of lieutenant governor, with the provision that he pledge himself to the Spanish cause. Bohórquez agreed to the terms. He then reveled in the week of celebrations given in his honor. He had a lot to celebrate—he had made himself king of the Calchaquí *and* a Spanish official.

For two years, he led a strong government for the Spanish, all the while building an army of indigenous warriors and fortifying the surrounding valleys against the Spanish. Dedicating himself to that work caused his relationship with the Spanish authorities to suffer, and inevitably, his duplicity was discovered. The governor tried to have him arrested, but Bohórquez turned to the Calchaquí, setting in motion a war.

The Spanish promised to forgive the Calchaquí for harboring a traitor if they would just turn him in, but despite Bohórquez's fraudulent claims to the Inca crown, they refused. A bloody battle ensued. Over two hundred indigenous warriors set upon Fort San Bernardo with ferocity, giving the Spanish a fight they would remember. Despite their courage, Bohórquez and the Calchaquí were defeated and withdrew.

Bohórquez knew he was in real trouble with the Spanish and audaciously begged for a pardon from the Spanish authorities in Salta. Even as he asked the Spanish for forgiveness and was being transported to Lima, he continued to foment uprisings among the native people.

The Spanish, tiring of his betrayals and constant trouble-making, eventually ran out of forgiveness for Bohórquez. Despite ridding themselves of the rebel leader, the Spanish troubles with the natives were not over. Jose Henriquez took up the cause and led the Quilmes into battle against the Spanish in 1665. This uprising, too, was put down and with dire consequences to the native people. In order to quash any future trouble from the indigenous tribes, the Spanish ordered that all eleven thousand natives be deported to the Pampean territories near Buenos Aires. The Quilmes people established a city there (the city of Quilmes), and it was there that they disappeared as an ethnic group.

The Third Calchaquí War continued for two more years with the last of the native Diaguita federations. After they were defeated by the Spanish, they were divided and deported, becoming slaves to the colonizers. The war ended on January 2nd, 1667, and on January 3rd, the Spanish secretly executed Bohórquez so as not to martyr him and give further cause for native uprisings. And so ended the third and final Calchaquí war.

As for the rest of the indigenous people, they found other ways to continue to survive. As settlements cropped up in the pampas, some tribes moved to remote locations in the vast land, areas colonists hadn't touched. Others married into settlements and were assimilated into the Spanish culture.

Only the Mapuche warrior tribe of Patagonia was never conquered by the Spanish; their fierce resistance and determination helped them to hold out against the long colonization campaign of the Spanish. But for the rest of the country, a new era was taking hold.

Chapter 6 – La Reconquista and La Defensa

While the revolution and bid for independence were coming to a close in North America in 1776, the ingredients for revolution in Argentina were just starting to come together. The native threat to the Spanish colony had been all but neutralized, and Spain had a surer foothold in the region. Argentina had just become incorporated into the new larger Spanish South American colony: the Viceroyalty of the Río de la Plata. However, Spain had neglected this territory in favor of dedicating resources to Peru, which was a greater source of wealth.

Around this time, Buenos Aires had grown into an important regional trading hub, with cattle products like hides, leather, tallow, and salted beef making up the bulk of the economy. However, the trade was not as lucrative as it might seem. Traders were taxed heavily, and strict regulations were imposed by the crown. Foreign trade was also off-limits; traders could only do business with Spain from the port in Lima, meaning that goods had to make an arduous trek across the Andes. This further restricted the city's economy, making trade difficult and expensive.

But legal trade was not the only business being conducted in the city. If the legal means of making money was difficult, there were those who would find a way around it, and they did. Buenos Aires became a haven for smugglers. Underground tunnels, many directly to the port, were used for illicit trading operations. The restrictions, the oppressive taxation, and the trouble it caused local traders began to water the seeds of rebellion, fostering a drive for political independence from the Spanish crown.

As Buenos Aires began to prosper economically, other major cities, like Córdoba, Rosario, and Santa Fe, became disillusioned and bitter due to having fewer economic opportunities. They felt that they were being robbed by Spain of their fair share of the trade. Being aware of the United States' successful war for independence, as well as France's revolution for equality, some Argentinians began to feel that they, too, would be better off free from the yoke of the Spanish crown. They began to question whether Spain had the right to control their affairs and if a fairer system could be enacted through an independent government that was actually present on the continent.

Much of the illegal trading out of Buenos Aires was done with the British. However, the British picked up more than just illicit products; they also picked up information and the general feel of the Argentinians toward Spain. The growing importance of the viceroyalty did not go unnoticed. Neither did what the British perceived as a weakness within the Spanish Empire. The British waited for the perfect moment to pounce.

That moment came on June 28th, 1806. When the British landed in the small bay of Ensenada de Barragán, the battle-hardened British soldiers may have expected to find a weak civil force, frightened without the help of mother Spain at their backs. This was reinforced when the inept Spanish viceroy, Rafael de Sobremonte, gathered his troops and, along with high-ranking Spanish commanders and wealthy Spanish merchants, fled across the Río de la Plata to Montevideo.

The fight would be left to Captain Santiago de Liniers, a small militia, and the people of the city. When the British landed, the Cabildo bell tolled, calling the inhabitants of Buenos Aires to arms. Artillery fire thundered into the bay. Manuel Belgrano, a former schoolmaster turned captain of the urban militias, reached the fortress, the assembly point to where the bell called. What he saw was disheartening. Groups of men, ignorant of organization and discipline, formed rudimentary companies, while others argued with the very viceroy they were supposed to defend. Belgrano knew right away that they were not prepared for battle.

Led by Liniers, the fledgling militia, adorned in their colorful uniforms and with banners waving, went up against the experienced combat veterans under the likes of commanders such as Brigadier General William Carr Beresford. Liniers, although having more skill with naval skirmishes than land battles, kept tight control over the movements of his own troops and those of the British. Still, the undisciplined militia was not able to beat back the more experienced British, and when the Argentinians had to retreat, Belgrano thought they had lost the city.

But reconvening after the retreat, the men under their lower-ranking creole (criollo) chiefs and officers began to move more efficiently and followed the proscribed tactics for battle, avoiding confusion and making their fight more effective.

Despite a few tactical errors on the part of Liniers, the Argentinians put up a fierce resistance, refusing to let the British take control of strategic points around the city. Failure to hold them back would have meant total defeat.

One such point was the fortress on the Plaza de Mayo, which did temporarily fall under British control. The fight to gain it back lasted for three days. But men were not the only ones who fought fiercely to regain the fortress. Manuela Hurtado y Pedraza fought at the side of her husband, an army corporal under Liniers. On the second day of the battle for the fortress, she watched as her husband was killed by a

British soldier. In recompense, she took her own bayonet and ran the soldier through, killing him. Flush with the heat of action, she immediately grabbed her dead husband's musket and continued fighting, killing at least one other British soldier.[20]

When the British capitulated just a week later, they had sustained heavy losses to their fighting force. While the militia of Buenos Aires counted their loss at 302 dead and 514 wounded (including 37 officers), the British troops were far worse off. About two thousand British were dead or wounded (a quarter of their soldiers), and more than one thousand had been taken prisoner. And so ended the battle that came to be called *La Reconquista de Buenos Aires* ("the reconquest of Buenos Aires").

After the battle, there was no way the people of Buenos Aires would allow the cowardly Rafael de Sobremonte, the man who had abandoned them on the brink of invasion, to return to his position as viceroy. Instead, in an unprecedented move, the *Real Audiencia de Buenos Aires* ("Royal Audience of Buenos Aires") deposed him and installed the heroic Santiago de Liniers as interim viceroy.[21] Never before had they deposed a viceroy without the express permission of the Spanish crown.

Liniers, for his part, was not going to let his guard down after the surprise British attack. As viceroy, he worked to arm the entire population of the city, including slaves. If another attack came, the city would be prepared to defend itself.

Despite their embarrassing defeat, the British were not put off for very long. Determined, they returned again in 1807, reinforced with ten times as many soldiers as before and with General John

---

[20] After the battle, Liniers appointed Manuela to the newly formed Patricians' Regiment, endowing her with the title of second lieutenant (*alférez*) and giving her a military salary.

[21] The *Real Audiencia de Buenos Aires* was the highest judiciary court of the Spanish crown in the viceroyalty.

Whitelocke leading the charge. This time, they would attempt to occupy the banks of the Río de la Plata.

Santiago de Liniers knew they were coming, and he and his troops waited for battle in an open field. The British, who would not be lured into open combat, took a more strategic route, marching across streams, mudflats, and between lagoons. Rather than looking to win a battle on the field, they set their sights on the city center.

Liniers took some of his troops and headed toward Miserere, an advantageous plaza that would give the British strategic access to the city. Upon reaching it, Liniers's troops were greeted with a sudden battle, causing their organized ranks to fall apart. The Argentinians were forced to withdraw, leaving the British with a well-located outpost in their hands. To the city's inhabitants, it appeared that all was lost.

Fortunately, Liniers felt differently. He had had the foresight to give advanced training to a regiment of troops, the Patricians' Regiment (*Regimiento de Patricios*), and had put them into the command of Colonel Cornelio de Saavedra. But they alone could not take back the city—all that were able would need to participate. They committed to battle readily. This included the mayor, Martín de Álzaga, who took on the mission to turn every corner near the Plaza Miserere into a reinforced trench.

After that, he turned to the Plaza Mayor and made it into a fortress, using it to defend the street from its windows and rooftops. In the streets themselves, cannons were brought in and protected with barricades while hundreds of riflemen converged on the square.

On July 5ᵗʰ, 1807, Whitelocke ordered thirteen columns of troops to converge and envelop Plaza Mayor. What they hadn't counted on was the inhabitants of Buenos Aires knowing their streets better than they did and using it to their advantage.

The entire city turned out to fight. Men and soldiers volleyed rifle shots and cannon fire in the streets. Family slaves, the elderly, women, and children threw everything they could—including boiling water, oil, and animal fat—at enemy forces from windows and roofs, reinforcing their own troops in the streets.

Some of the women used more deceptive means to help defeat the British. Martina Céspedes owned a grocery store in the city. She and her daughters decided to take down as many soldiers as possible. When the English went looking for alcoholic drinks, she and her daughters lured them into the basement of their shop. There, they plied the soldiers with food and alcohol until they fell drunk. In all, they captured twelve soldiers before handing them over to Liniers.[22,23]

Around the plaza, hundreds of redcoats lay dead within minutes, and the toll continued to mount into the thousands. The Argentinians called for Whitelocke to surrender. He refused, which was a mistake. The British could not overcome the organization, advanced knowledge of the city, and the fervor of every inhabitant to defend it.

Outnumbered ten thousand to seven thousand, the inhabitants of Buenos Aires held off the British with surprising strength. On July 7th, Whitelocke relented. He surrendered to Liniers and signed a treaty. The British army had lost 2,500 men during the battle that came to be known as *La Defensa* ("the Defense").[24]

Aside from ridding themselves of the British invaders, many of the Argentinian-born began to see things differently. They successfully fended off attacks without any help from Spain, and that strength

---

[22] Legend had it that she only handed over eleven of the troops, reserving one to marry her daughter Josefa.

[23] For her part in the battle, Céspedes was named "Defender of Buenos Aires" and was made a sergeant major in the army, complete with pay and uniform, which was used mainly for ceremonial purposes.

[24] Buenos Aires lost 1,600 men in the battle.

continued to water the seeds of independence among the region. The idea of a self-governed Buenos Aires began to be debated.[25]

---

[25] At the time, Buenos Aires was the capital of the Viceroyalty of the Río de la Plata. Among the territories the viceroyalty encompassed were the present-day countries of Argentina, Paraguay, Uruguay, and Bolivia.

Chapter 7 – The Path Toward Independence

Another crack in the Spanish Empire came in 1808. Napoleon Bonaparte invaded Spain, deposing and imprisoning King Ferdinand VII and putting his brother Joseph on the throne. Ferdinand would be kept under guard by the French for six years. During that time, tensions began to mount between Argentinian-born colonists (criollos) and Spanish troops, who were uneasy at the thought of being half a world away from Spain, unable to assist the troubled crown.

Without their royal central government, Spain and its new colonies would descend into confusion over who was in charge. Localities created juntas: administrative councils formed to rule in the absence of royal authority. One of these emerged in Seville, Spain—the Supreme Central Junta—and it claimed authority over the Spanish colonies in the Indies. This included the Viceroyalty of the Río de la Plata, which covered Argentina.

It was only a matter of time before the news reached Buenos Aires that its mother country had been weakened by the king's imprisonment. The newly formed junta had no royal backing, and questions arose over how much authority it had over the territory. Things began to stir.

Santiago de Liniers's administration was still in effect at this time, and it was popular with Argentinian-born residents. But not everyone was happy with his rule. The governor of Montevideo, Francisco Javier de Elío, and a merchant named Martín de Álzaga (the same Álzaga who was the mayor during *La Defensa*) were two such prominent dissenters. Though they would not outright oppose Liniers as viceroy, de Elío created the Junta of Montevideo, a government that would decide when and if they would obey orders from Liniers's administration in Buenos Aires. It was not an outright rebellion, but it was just the beginning.

Three criollo intellectuals entered the scene.[26] Mariano Moreno, Bernardino Rivadavia, and Manuel Belgrano had been inspired by the liberal thinking of some European countries. They were unhappy with the old order and poured their energy into restructuring the old colonial ways in order to form a new nation with a new order. This did not sit well with the colonial administrators, large landowners, rich merchants, and clergymen, all of whom benefited greatly from the old ways and were perfectly happy to keep them. They were not about to let their privileged status be tampered with and would violently oppose any changes. But after the rich Spanish merchants and other prominent Spanish men left the criollos in the city high and dry during the British invasions, they were not allowed to have the same clout that they enjoyed before. A separation between the Spanish-born and Argentinian-born whites became wider. The tide was turning, with power favoring the creole population.

On January 1st, 1809, Álzaga greeted the new year with mutiny. Determined to get Liniers removed from his position, he held a meeting of prominent individuals in the city. Álzaga demanded that Liniers resign and that a local junta be appointed. The Spanish militia and many locals, including some criollos, showed up and supported

---

[26] Criollos (or creoles) were Argentine-born Spanish or Europeans, oftentimes with mixed indigenous blood. The term is no longer used in Latin America except in reference to this time period.

this rebellion.[27] But many of the criollos distrusted Álzaga's motives and did not believe he wanted change; they thought he only wanted to keep his own authority. A riotous mutiny ensued.

Cornelio de Saavedra and his criollo militia quickly stepped in to squash the riot, surrounding the plaza and forcing the rebels, including the Spanish militia, to disarm and disperse. The mutinous leaders were then exiled, and the power of the Argentinian criollos increased.[28]

Although the rebellion was quickly put down, Liniers was still going to be replaced. The Supreme Central Junta decided on Baltasar Hidalgo de Cisneros, a war veteran, to replace Liniers as the viceroy of Río de la Plata. Belgrano pressed Liniers to resist. As far as he was concerned, Liniers had been confirmed in his position by Spain's king, whereas Cisneros had not; he had only been appointed by the Supreme Central Junta. The criollo militias agreed with Belgrano. Despite the support, Liniers peacefully handed over the reins of the viceroyalty to Cisneros in June 1809. This angered the entire criollo population of the city. They believed that the Spanish forced Liniers out in order to install someone more loyal to the crown, reestablishing political domination and trade monopoly.

Cisneros did not disappoint Spain. Perhaps in a show of loyalty to the crown, he, in short order, rearmed the recently disbanded Spanish militia and pardoned the mutineers who went against Liniers. However, he also wanted a conciliatory relationship with the city's criollos, whom he knew viewed him with suspicion. With the city's economy in grave crisis, he came up with a solution that would surely make the criollos happy—allowing free trade.

---

[27] This included Moreno, who was seen as one of the leaders of the rebellion.

[28] The exiles were later freed by de Elío and given political asylum in Montevideo.

Chapter 8 – The May Revolution

The next year, free trade brought important news to Buenos Aires—news that was about to tip the scales. On May 14th, 1810, a British ship arrived with newspapers from Europe. The news it contained would help launch a series of events that would rock the colony and touch off the tension that had been broiling underneath the surface of Buenos Aires.

Seville, the seat of the Supreme Central Junta, had been invaded by the French Army in January. The junta that had connected Buenos Aires to Spain's government had been dissolved, with its members fleeing to Isla de León.

On May 17th, the news was confirmed by newspapers that arrived in Montevideo via a British ship. Reports came into Buenos Aires that the displaced Supreme Central Junta members had not been idle. While on Isla de León, they quickly formed the Council of Regents in Cádiz. Unlike the more progressive junta, the new council wanted to restore absolute sovereignty, meaning that Spain's government would have complete control over the affairs in Buenos Aires and the viceroyalty.

This news did not sit well. The people knew either the French would have a victory over Spain or the absolute government of Spain would be restored. Neither option was appealing to the South Americans.

Unnerved by the prospects, Cisneros did everything in his power to keep the news from getting out. He monitored British ships that came to port and immediately seized newspapers that reported European developments, hoping to contain the news. News of this magnitude could not be contained, however.

This information soon fell into the hands of Belgrano and revolutionary military leader Juan José Castelli. The men quickly spread the news to other patriots around the city. It was just what the patriots needed to hear to spur them to action. And it was just what Cisneros feared. Having been appointed viceroy and backed by a junta that no longer existed, Cisneros no longer had a leg to stand on. The people of Buenos Aires saw their long-awaited opportunity, and they were going to seize it. The May Revolution was about to begin.

As news of the French victory in Spain spread among the city's residents, so did their uneasiness. Shops closed as military activity increased. But that did not stop the meetings among the people to discuss the political situation. Some meetings gave rise to radical proclamations, even prompting one prominent citizen to call for Cisneros to be hanged in public. However, with weapons being barred from leaving the barracks, violence was kept at bay.

Cisneros tried desperately to calm the rising tension among the people. He would not confirm that the junta had been dissolved but asked the people to continue their allegiance to the imprisoned King Ferdinand. The people were not pacified. Tensions intensified within the city, especially among the patriots.

Cisneros continued to grasp for a solution to appease the growing rumblings to cut ties with Spain. He proposed creating a proxy government to rule on behalf of the Spanish crown, a government comprised of current leaders of the viceroyalty. The criollos, who were disenchanted with the current leadership that was already carrying out Spain's bidding, knew this proposal would be a lateral move. They were not buying it.

Secret meetings continued at the house of wealthy businessman Nicolás Rodríguez Peña, as well as at the house of Martín Rodríguez, a resistance fighter during the 1806 and 1807 British invasions. Rodríguez wanted to depose the viceroy in a show of force. But Cornelio de Saavedra and Castelli, being more moderate revolutionaries, wanted to avoid a violent overthrow if possible. They proposed an open cabildo, a town hall meeting, instead. There would be no need for force as long as the viceroy willingly granted them permission to meet.

They were not going to leave support during the cabildo to chance, however. They were going to enter that town hall meeting prepared. On the night of Saturday, May 19th, the men agreed to meet with various local administrators, military leaders, and prominent citizens to ask for their support at the cabildo.

Once support was gathered, they would make a show of requesting permission from the viceroy to allow the open cabildo to take place. They would let him know that should he refuse to allow the cabildo, criollo troops would be mobilized to march on the viceroy in the plaza, and they would force him to resign by violence if necessary. They would then replace him with their own government. In reality, they were leaving Cisneros little choice in the matter. Allow them to convene or face a major rebellion.

They sent municipal magistrate Juan José de Lezica to deliver the news and persuade the viceroy to concede. To pressure him to get the job done and get it done fast, the patriots let Lezica know they already found him suspicious and that any delay or failure on his part would force them to consider him a traitor. Lezica agreed to the task but not without issuing a dire warning. If they didn't get permission and decided to depose the viceroy with a show of force, they would be marked as rebels and outlaws. Undeterred, Manuel Belgrano told him to let the viceroy know he had until the following Monday, two days, to decide. They were not going to wait indefinitely for an answer.

Cisneros was informed of the request on Sunday, May 20th. He feared that the cabildo was a trap. He summoned military commanders and demanded support. He wanted the military to guard the fort and take all keys to the entrances of the meeting hall so as not to allow himself to be locked in. Unfortunately for Cisneros, Colonel Cornelio de Saavedra was in command of the criollo regiments, and he was staunchly on the side of the Argentinian-born patriots.

Being fully aware of Napoleon's position over Spain, Saavedra announced to Cisneros that he would not recognize any authority of the Council of Regents in Cádiz. They had no power to reach them in the Americas, and the local army was better off looking after themselves. He also did not fail to make it clear to Cisneros that he no longer recognized his authority as viceroy either. With the Supreme Central Junta gone, so was the legitimacy of Cisneros's position. Because of that, he refused to give Cisneros the military support for which he asked.

In fact, another commander was going to ensure that Cisneros could not call for support during the meeting. Juan Florencio Terrada and his Infantry of Grenadiers, being conveniently barracked below Cisneros's office window, were in a prime position to prevent any other regiments from coming to Cisneros's aid during the meeting with Castelli and Rodríguez. Terrada's forces would also be there to make sure that Cisneros didn't try to capture the criollo representatives and imprison them.

When Castelli and Rodríguez arrived for their meeting, Cisneros put on a show of nonchalance. Finding him casually playing cards with three other men when they pushed their way in unannounced, they demanded that Cisneros allow them to have an open cabildo. Cisneros became outraged, but Rodríguez would not back down; he demanded an answer. After consulting with his aide, Cisneros reluctantly agreed.

While the meeting took place, a number of revolutionaries attended a play titled *Rome Saved*. During the last act, the leading man gave a rousing speech about the need for strong leadership. Though he was in character and was reciting what was in the script, the speech touched a chord with the revolutionaries in attendance, and they applauded heartily. Theologian and lawyer-turned-revolutionary-leader Juan José Paso was in attendance. He was so stirred by the scene that he stood up and shouted for the freedom of Buenos Aires, causing a fight to break out.

The revolutionaries who had attended the play followed up by going to Peña's house, not knowing the outcome of the meeting with Cisneros. There, they were informed of Cisneros's consent. But they did not trust his word. Worried that he would renege on his agreement, they planned a demonstration to show Cisneros that they meant business and to ensure he kept true to his word.

The next day, Monday, May 21st, a portrait of Ferdinand VII could be seen coming down the street. The six hundred men behind it, ominously calling themselves the Infernal Legion, marched behind the portrait with white ribbons on their jackets, symbolizing Spanish-criollo unity. Leading the pack was a city mail courier and treasury department worker. When they reached the town hall, their shouts thundered across the Plaza de la Victoria. They demanded that Cisneros resign his position as viceroy. They did not trust his agreement from the night before, and Belgrano led the call for a firm commitment to the open cabildo.

Watching from the barracks, Saavedra paced nervously. Rumors were swirling that Cisneros was dead and that he, Saavedra, would seize control of the government. Though he knew it wasn't true, the rumors and the violent air of the riotous demonstration concerned him deeply. He also knew that the situation was tricky. He feared an assassination attempt on Cisneros, yet attempting to stop the demonstration would likely cause the troops to mutiny.

Meanwhile, Belgrano faced a similar sticky scenario. He was asked to help prepare for the meeting, and he thought doing so would help the crowd see it as a guarantee of it happening. Yet, in going over the guest list the members of the city council had created, Belgrano saw trouble. Only wealthy citizens had been invited, leaving the poor to remain outside and unrepresented. They were stacking the list with people favorable toward Cisneros. Belgrano knew that was asking for further unrest. His protests went unheeded, and when the council members tried to persuade him to support Cisneros, Belgrano left. The invitations went out to the 450 prominent citizens and officials on their carefully crafted guest list.

Belgrano left the cabildo because he was angry about the unfairness toward the common people. The crowd, not knowing the reason that he left, were angered at what they thought was his betrayal. Was he no longer working for their cause? Worried about Belgrano's departure, the crowd turned from calling for Cisneros's resignation to demanding the open town hall meeting—their original plan.

The tension in the plaza was becoming too much for Saavedra, so he decided to act. Knowing the people were looking for support, he assured the Infernal Legion that the military was behind their cause. This settled the minds of the raucous crowd, and to Saavedra's relief, they dispersed.

Having been informed of the city council's heavily biased guest list, the revolutionaries decided to remedy that by sending invitations to a guest list of their own. Agustín Donado, the printer in charge of making the invitations, was sympathetic to the revolutionary cause, and at their behest, he printed excess invitations that they could distribute to whom they chose. They hoped that they could get invitations into the hands of enough criollos to turn the tide against Cisneros during the meeting the following day.

Out of the 450 on the official guest list, only about 250 showed up to the open cabildo on Tuesday, May 22nd. But the criollos did not fail to show up. And they took measures to ensure that the meeting would have a criollo majority in attendance. Six hundred armed men came to the plaza and stationed themselves in a position that allowed them to control access to the town hall.

Though prominent citizens, militia commanders, and religious leaders of the town showed up, some expressed their doubts and outright fears about the meeting. Some worried that no matter what the outcome of the meeting would be, violence would ensue between those with opposing views. Some prominent Spanish-born residents also feared that with too many criollos in attendance, the meeting would lack legitimacy. Despite these fears, the meeting began.

The meeting lasted the entire day. The focus of the debate was over the legitimacy of the Supreme Central Junta-appointed viceroy and the Spanish-controlled government. Those in favor of independence heavily questioned the principle of retroversion of sovereignty to the people and how it applied to the situation in the colony.[29] With the king imprisoned by Napoleon, Spain had applied the retroversion principle in appointing juntas to rule, which were legitimate actions.

Here, however, was where the criollos felt things got questionable. They argued that the colonies were considered direct possessions of the king of Spain, not colonies belonging to the country or its government. Therefore, only the king or his appointed viceroys had any direct say over the colonies' affairs. They concluded, then, that any appointments in Buenos Aires made by Seville's Supreme Central Junta or subsequent Council of Regents were illegitimate as the colony was not their possession, nor did they have any jurisdiction over its

---

[29] This principle, as applied to Spain at the time, stated that if the monarch or legitimate royal authority was not present or unable to rule (as was here in the case of the imprisoned Ferdinand VII), sovereign power returned to the people, who had the right to appoint new government leadership.

affairs. Since Cisneros was not appointed by the king or a representative viceroy, he had no legitimate authority.

The meeting was divided, the rivalry between the Spanish "Peninsulars" and native-born criollos becoming ever more apparent.[30] The criollos and revolutionaries supported this line of reasoning and called to replace the viceroy with a junta of their own choosing. The Peninsulars thought that things should remain in place, given the unprecedented nature of the situation. They believed that as long as a Spaniard laid foot on the soil, the territory was rightfully under Spanish command.

Some took a more moderate stance. Castelli, for example, stated that the people should take control of the government until a legitimate monarch returned to the throne. In his speech, he appealed to the logic of those present, stating:

"Nobody could call the whole nation a criminal, nor the individuals that have aired their political views. If the right of conquest belongs by right to the conquering country, it would be fair for Spain to quit resisting the French and submit to them, by the same principles for which it is expected that the Americans submit themselves to the peoples of Pontevedra. The reason and the rule must be equal for everybody. Here there are no conquerors or conquered; here there are only Spaniards. The Spaniards of Spain have lost their land. The Spaniards of America are trying to save theirs. Let the ones from Spain deal with themselves as they can; do not worry, we American Spaniards know what we want and where we go. So, I suggest we vote that we replace the Viceroy with a new authority that will be subject to the parent state if it is saved from the French."[31]

---

[30] Colonial residents of Argentina who had been born in Spain

[31] Translated from Spanish.

Others took a similar stance, suggesting that the town council have provisional control of Buenos Aires and the viceroyalty until a junta with representatives from all over the region could be established. Some proposed that the junta could be headed by Cisneros himself.

Still, the debate raged on until midnight, with the attendants heavily divided. Belgrano, anticipating trouble, stood by the window at the ready. One wave of his white cloth and the armed men gathered in the plaza would storm their way into the building.

Fortunately, there was no need for Belgrano to wave his flag. Mariano Moreno, however, sensed trouble. Although the meeting had achieved a majority vote, won by those in favor of ousting Cisneros and forming a junta, the victory was not secure. Moreno turned to writer and Freemason Vincente López y Planes and told him the town council was about to betray them.

But when daylight dawned on Wednesday, May 23rd, 1810, the town council of Buenos Aires announced to the city that Cisneros would no longer be in charge. The council would hold temporary authority until a junta could be formed and power transferred to that ruling body. Despite the victory, they were not out of the woods yet. Notices were posted around the city, asking the people for peace in accord with the will of the majority who had voted.

The town council, now in control, was going to do things their own way. They would form a temporary junta until representatives from other areas could arrive, and they would appoint Cisneros as the president of the temporary junta, as well as the commander of the military. The name of his position of authority may have changed, but Cisneros would still be in charge. His opposers could not be happy, especially with two other Peninsulars also being appointed to the junta. But there was a bright spot—Castelli and Saavedra were also appointed to be on the junta.

No one, not even Cisneros, would hold absolute power. A constitution was created to regulate how much power the junta had and how much power any one man within it could wield. Although Cisneros was named president, the constitutional code would not allow him to do anything without the agreement of the others. It would also give the town council a certain amount of power, allowing them to dismiss any members who were not performing their duties properly.

New tax laws would also be created by the junta, an important move considering that taxes to Spain, along with the stifling of commerce, had long been the major causes for calls for independence.

It was also agreed that the town council would send invitations to other cities for delegates to join the new junta, ensuring that all areas would have representation in the new government. The two military commanders in the city, one of whom was Saavedra, agreed to all the things proposed in the constitutional code. Later that day, Thursday, May 24th, the new temporary junta was officially sworn into office.

The revolutionaries were shaken to their core by what had occurred. Although the new constitutional code stated that those who attended the town meeting and had been in opposition to the changes would be granted amnesty and that they would not have to fear reprisals from the new government, the revolutionaries feared punishment. They even began to have doubts about members of their cause, like Castelli and Saavedra, who had agreed and supported these new developments. Despite the council's call for peace, more unrest followed.

A mob gathered in the plaza square. They were outraged that Cisneros still had power. Even though it was limited, they saw it as an affront to the feelings of those who had attended the open meeting. They were outraged. Colonel Martín Rodríguez stepped up with a dire warning. He proclaimed that "everyone without exception" demanded Cisneros be ousted from the new government and that if he wasn't, there would be a revolt. The military would be obliged to put it down, firing on their own people, which would only serve to make the situation more explosive. The tension in the city was palpable.

Wanting to avoid a violent revolution, Castelli and Saavedra resigned from the new junta that night. But that would not be enough, and they strongly suggested that Cisneros resign as well. It would be the only way to truly appease the mob. Castelli and Saavedra warned them that if Cisneros refused to resign, they would be powerless to stop the violent mutiny that would be sure to follow. Cisneros wavered in his decision, wanting to wait for the next day to commit one way or the other. But with the situation so volatile, the men felt that he could not delay in making the decision.

The next day, Friday, May 25th, Cisneros submitted his resignation to the town council, but they had yet to confirm it. Some revolutionary leaders were encouraged by the resignations of Castelli and Saavedra. Moreno, disgusted with the unexpected developments, washed his hands of the whole matter—he was done.

The people of the city, however, were not done with the matter and would not rest until the outcome was to their liking. A crowd gathered, despite the foul weather that morning, undeterred by the rain. It wasn't enough that Cisneros had handed in his resignation—there were fears that the city council would reject it. In their eyes, it wouldn't be a done deal until the resignation was confirmed.

And now, even the resignation of Cisneros would not be enough for the people of the city. They loudly demanded that the newly elected junta be dissolved and that a new one, sans Cisneros, be appointed.

When the official announcement of Cisneros's resignation was delayed, the agitation of the people grew. Shouts went up in the plaza, demanding that they be told what was happening. It wasn't even 9 a.m., and the city was already on the verge of an uproar. What followed would do nothing to quell the simmering rage.

When the town council finally met at 9 a.m., they rejected Cisneros's resignation. They would not pander to the people, who they considered to have no right or say over who the city council chose for the junta. It had already been decided, and they would not turn back on their decision.

Knowing the reaction that this decision would evoke, they agreed that a riot would have to be stopped by force. The city's top military commanders were summoned. They refused to show up, including Saavedra. Their explanation for disobeying orders? They would not support the government or their order. If they were commanded to fire upon the demonstrators outside, they would unequivocally refuse.

Outside, the situation among the crowd continued to simmer. With tensions boiling over, they stormed the chapter house. Hoping to stave off violence, Lezica asked for the crowd to send a spokesperson who could go in and express the will of the people. Five men were sent to go, but one of them, Pancho Planes, a known rioter, was marked as potential trouble. Authorities tried to dissuade him from going in, but he ignored them and marched into the hall with the others.

The city council firmly stated that the people of Buenos Aires had no right to change the political system of the entire region. The other provinces had the right to have a say. The spokesmen argued that delegates had been called and would be considered for the new permanent junta. Deliberations between the two sides continued. It was again emphasized that should the people rise up and riot against Cisneros, military troops would not help. They would mutiny if ordered to use force.

Rodríguez, one of the spokesmen who went into the hall, pointed out to the city council that without military backing, their acceptance of Cisneros's resignation was the only way to stop the crowd that was clamoring just outside their doors. Julían de Leyva, the procurator of the town council, convinced the other members to reconsider. With the sounds of a near revolt on the other side of the door, the other members were finally persuaded to accept Cisneros's resignation. At that, the crowd returned to the plaza. But they were not going to be quieted that easily.

Seizing on the temporary power vacuum this had created, the crowd wasted no time continuing to push for what they wanted. They again stormed into the town hall and made their way to the hall of deliberations. Revolutionary militia leader Antonio Beruti stepped up to speak. He told the city council that the people demanded that they have a say in electing the new junta. He informed them that this was no empty or idle demand. Aside from the four hundred people currently behind him, the military was full of soldiers in support of the revolutionary actions. All were ready to take control of the election, even if it meant by force. Perhaps to buy themselves some time to deal with the intensity of the situation, the town council asked for their demands in writing.

A document complete with 411 signatures was drafted and given to the council. With the patience of the rain-soaked people in the plaza wearing thin, any further delay would result in a violent outbreak. The council accepted the terms of the document and, from the balcony, read it aloud to the people in the plaza. Those present eagerly called out their consent and immediately ratified the document. In the next moment, something incredible happened.

The rain suddenly stopped, and the sun burst through the clouds. The people saw this as a divine omen. It came to be known as the Sun of May.[32]

---

[32] The Sun of May became a national symbol for Argentina, with a representation of it being at the center of the Argentinian flag.

And so, the Primera Junta was created. Cornelio de Saavedra was elected president of the Primera Junta, with Manuel Belgrano, Juan José Castelli, and Mariano Moreno being among the members. Other members included Brigadier General Miguel de Azcuénaga, priest Manuel Alberti, Spanish-born Argentine businessmen Domingo Matheu, Spanish businessman Juan Larrea, and secretary Juan José Paso.

Despite the victory, there had been no formal declaration of independence. The Primera Junta was still ruling in the name of King Ferdinand VII. For the people of the viceroyalty, the war for independence was not over; it was just beginning. And Cisneros was not going to go down quietly.

Chapter 9 – The War for Independence Gains Ground

In Córdoba, Santiago de Liniers saw a postrider come with an urgent message. It was from Baltasar Hildago de Cisneros, and it contained a warning. Cisneros informed Liniers of the events that had passed during the week of the May Revolution in Buenos Aires. The old government had dissolved, and a new one had sprung up, ousting him from his appointed position. He needed Liniers's help—he wanted Liniers to raise the viceroyalty's military against the new Primera Junta.

Liniers, Córdoba governor Juan Gutiérrez de la Concha, and the city's elites discussed the situation. The Council of Regents refused to sanction and recognize the Primera Junta, and the *Real Audiencia de Buenos Aires* ("Royal Audience of Buenos Aires"), along with the Peninsulars, followed suit. Unlike the revolutionaries of Buenos Aires, Córdoba decided to recognize the authority of the Council of Regents in Cádiz. They believed the new junta of Buenos Aires should too. Liniers would begin the counter-revolution. He wrote to royalists in other cities, requesting military support so he could go up against the junta.

Back in Buenos Aires, the Primera Junta knew that Córdoba was its most dangerous enemy. The Primera Junta sent an army, commanded by Francisco Ortiz de Ocampo, to fight against the counter-revolutionary force gathering in Córdoba. Meanwhile, the Primera Junta had another persistent problem on their hands—Cisneros.

Cisneros had been furiously writing to various cities and councils within the viceroyalty, working fast to try to garner support against the new government of the Primera Junta. To his intense dismay, all but Córdoba supported the new junta. Thus, the counter-revolution he started with Liniers was weakly supported. They could only rely on the strength of Córdoba.

The Primera Junta caught wind of Cisneros's sedition. Avoiding an all-out confrontation, they employed deception in order to catch him. The members of the junta told Cisneros and the Royal Audience that their lives were in danger and had Cisneros gather them, ostensibly for their protection. But it was a trap. They captured the men and immediately set them aboard a ship, exiling them to the Canary Islands. Now they could focus their attention on Córdoba.

Ocampo and his army went to meet the approaching army that Liniers had gathered. They were prepared for a battle and were surprised when they did not have to fight one. As Liniers's troops neared Buenos Aires, their courage failed them. Liniers was deserted by many of his soldiers. The army was further damaged by infiltrators loyal to the new junta.

Liniers knew the jig was up, and along with other counter-revolutionary leaders, he tried to run from Ocampo and his army. Ocampo caught every last one of them. But now, he was in a bit of a bind as to what to do with the captives. Knowing that they, especially Liniers, were popular figures, he did not want to risk further violence by executing them. It also went against his conscience to execute a priest, as Rodrigo de Orellana, the bishop of Córdoba, was captured. Instead, Ocampo handed them over to Buenos Aires.

The Primera Junta feared the popularity of Liniers as well. As the junta did not want him in the city to stir up supporters, it would not allow the prisoners to enter. Instead, Castelli went to deal with the situation himself. But first, he had to deal with Ocampo. When sending Castelli off, Moreno said to him, "Go, Castelli, and I hope you will not incur the same weakness as our general, if not yet fulfilled the determination, Larrea will go, and finally I'll go myself if necessary." Ocampo did not stand a chance.

Castelli arrived and had Ocampo demoted and replaced. He then ordered that the executions be carried out at Cabeza de Tigre. Liniers was among the executed by gunfire. The junta, afraid of making a heretical action, spared Bishop Orellana and sent him into exile.

Getting rid of Liniers, Cisneros, and the Royal Audience did not solve the problems plaguing the Primera Junta. The new government, which was still technically tied to the crown as a ruling representative, did not present the people with the clear leadership that existed in other areas. One of the founding members, Moreno, was removed from office shortly after its establishment. Castelli, going into Córdoba after its defeat, was not well received in the city. And old rivalries with Montevideo flared.

The Primera Junta sent Castelli and others on military campaigns to gain support for the new government. Uruguay, of which Montevideo is the capital, was not the only province that did not want to be under the control of the new autonomous government in Buenos Aires. Peru and Asunción (Paraguay) also bucked, challenging their authority. Battles raged between the central government in Buenos Aires and the other regions, which fought for their own autonomy. What followed was a multi-faceted war with various regions battling for independence. Spurred by Argentina's bid for independence, these regions could not be stopped in the quest for their own.

Despite delegates from other provinces joining and enlarging the ruling body of the Primera Junta (renamed the Junta Grande), disunity in the region continued. With the Spanish authority that held them together disappearing, the viceroyalty splintered.

Military defeats, such as the one fought at Huaqui in June 1811, crushed the morale of the Argentine Army. Led by Castelli, the revolutionary force attacked the royalist army with slingshots and grenades, backed up by cavalry and muskets. The battle ended with the revolutionary army retreating so quickly that they left most of their artillery on the battlefield, along with one thousand of their dead. The defeat spelled the beginning of the end for Castelli.

The Junta Grande's prestige suffered greatly after the defeat at Huaqui. It was the final blow for the waning body. With Saavedra in Upper Peru commanding the Army of the North, liberal factions sprung at the chance to dissolve the junta. The First Triumvirate sprung up in its place, led by Feliciano Chiclana, Juan José Paso, and Manuel de Sarratea. They held power over what was now called the United Provinces of the Río de la Plata.

The Triumvirate set its sights on Castelli. The members of the new Triumvirate, who were confined in Catamarca, blamed him for the debacle at Huaqui. There would be a trial to hold him accountable. Isolated and with political support waning, Castelli stood trial. The tongue cancer that was ravaging his mouth made it hard for him to speak, let alone defend himself. He died on October 12th, 1812, while still on trial.

Earlier in the year, the Triumvirate replaced Castelli with Belgrano as the commander of the Army of the North. Colonel José de San Martín, a war veteran who had turned his back on Spain to answer the call of his native Argentina, went along with Belgrano to Jujuy Province. The situation there quickly became alarming.

With the royalist army bearing down on the city of San Salvador de Jujuy, it crushed every revolutionary regiment in its path. With three thousand or more soldiers in their ranks, the royalist army formed an imposing force, one that the revolutionaries felt was impossible to beat. That was when Belgrano decided to use scorched earth tactics.

He knew that with the royalists approaching, his army would have to withdraw or face certain defeat. But if the royalists captured the city without a fight, it would provide them with much-needed supplies like food, shelter, and livestock. Belgrano was not about to just hand that out to the enemy. He asked the people of Jujuy to do the unthinkable.

Calling on their courage to do what they could think of as their patriotic duty, he asked them to leave their homes, carrying with them all the supplies that they could, and flee to the city of Tucumán. Anything that was left behind or they saw on their way to Tucumán that could be useful to the enemy army was to be destroyed. The city rose to the call, even though it meant leaving in the dead of winter.[33]

The people burned it all—homes, crops, and anything else that might assist the enemy forces. After destroying what they could, they would have to leave quickly, with the royalist army only a day or two away. The arduous trip to Tucumán would take days.

Of the 3,000 inhabitants, 1,500 of them left in carts, on the backs of their donkeys, or on foot. The rest, mainly those of the wealthy upper class, hid or ran to other locations. No one wanted to remain when the enemy army arrived. This event became known as the Jujuy Exodus.[34]

The danger was not over, however. A month later, the Spanish would follow Belgrano and the displaced citizens of San Salvador de Jujuy to the refuge in Tucumán. A battle ensued, but the Army of the North was ready for them. They forced the royalist army to retreat,

---

[33] August 22nd and 23rd, 1812.

[34] Sometimes also referenced as the *Éxodo Jujeño.*

and eventually, they defeated them in the Battle of Salta. Six months later, the people of Jujuy were able to return to their decimated lands. It was time to rebuild.

The war for independence did not end there. The people of San Salvador de Jujuy would have to repel advances by the royalist army ten more times. But elsewhere, after helping the residents of Jujuy flee to safety and then winning the Battle of Tucumán, a new national hero was emerging.

Chapter 10 – "Hannibal of the Andes"

José de San Martín was only seven when his father was recalled from Argentina to return to Spain. He hardly had time to form many memories of the country of his birth before leaving it. Back in Spain, he went to a seminary school, but the military was his real calling. By age eleven, he had joined the army as a cadet, and at seventeen, the young lieutenant had already seen action in France and against the Moors in Algeria. He would see several other battles with the Spanish Army, including the War of the Oranges against the Portuguese and, in Spain, against Napoleon, repelling the French invasion. He would also be captured in battle and returned during a prisoner exchange. In 1804, he was made a captain in the Spanish Army.

So, by the time 1811 came, San Martín had quite the resume as a war veteran. But it was in that year that he looked back toward the Spanish colonies in South America, particularly Argentina, and decided to defect to the revolutionaries to aid in their fight for independence.

After helping Belgrano at Jujuy and Tucumán, it was time for San Martín's baptism by fire. A settlement along the Paraná River had long been harassed by the Spanish royalist armies, and Colonel San Martín was sent to take care of it.

Before he went, however, he was going to make sure that his military unit was properly trained to his liking. Having gained knowledge of Napoleon's military tactics while fighting his army in Spain, San Martín now trained his own troops with these same modern techniques.

Once they were ready, the regiment moved to Rosario. There, he and 120 of his men moved under cover of darkness, following the Spanish ships. When San Martín found out the royalists planned to invade the San Carlos Convent, he quickly moved into action, driving his forces to reach it first. Celedonio Escalada, San Martín's second-in-command, split from San Martín with a smaller column of troops under his command. He reached the convent before San Martín, who was marching toward them with the majority of the army. Despite their efforts at maintaining the element of surprise, an unavoidable clue gave their location away. The royalist army, part of whom were sitting in ships on the river, could see the dust Escalada and his men kicked up as they marched to the convent.

Escalada soon discovered the royalist ship. After setting up their cannon, they fired, only to miss. The ship sat safely out of range. Escalada and his troops were forced to fall back. However, a lucky break was about to come their way.

A Paraguayan prisoner escaped the royalist ship and was found by Escalada and his men. He told them that the royalist force currently sitting in the river was not all they would have to contend with. A much larger force was on its way to the convent, probably with an eye on stealing the money they thought was kept there.

The news of a larger army approaching stopped Escalada in his tracks. He went back to San Martín to report what he had heard. San Martín and his forces would need to hurry if they were to have any chance at beating the coming royalist army to the now deserted convent. San Martín formulated a plan to speed up their approach in which Ángel Pacheco would be sent ahead of the rest of the regiment. He was ordered to prepare horses at various relay points, saving the army valuable time.

Within two days, the entire army made it to the convent. Entering through the rear door, they hid inside without making fires or noise to give themselves away. They watched and waited. San Martín went to the belfry tower and, using his monocular, watched the royalist army's every move.

San Martín knew he couldn't attack the ships. The flat plains surrounding the convent would mean that a surprise attack would be out of the question, but it was a good location for the cavalry to maneuver. As he continued to study the battlefield, he also noticed that there was just one small path from the enemy ships to the open fields. If they could force the enemy to retreat down the narrow path, they would surely bottleneck, giving them the advantage from the rear. Yet, the royalists would have long-range guns on the ship to protect them. San Martín would need to think his strategy through thoroughly.

As the sun was just beginning to rise on the day of the battle, San Martín had his grenadiers slip out of the convent and get into battle formation behind the building. Still wanting to rely on the element of surprise, he split the cavalry into two regiments so they could flank the enemy on both sides.

Using only sabers and spears, the cavalry mounted their attack, with San Martín leading the charge. With surprise and speed on their side, the cavalrymen quickly outmaneuvered the royalists and their heavy cannons.

In the heat of battle, San Martín suddenly felt his horse falling out from under him. Soon, he was trapped under the dead weight of his five-hundred-pound horse. A royalist soldier saw this and did not waste the opportunity to try to kill him while he lay incapacitated. However, he missed his head and shot him in the arm. Not wasting time to reload his firearm, the royalist then drew his saber and struck San Martín in the face. Just before he could deal the final blow, two grenadiers came to San Martín's rescue, saving his life.

After a mere fifteen minutes of fighting, forty royalists were dead or injured, including their commander, Antonio Zabala. Argentine fighter Hippolyte Bouchard killed the Spanish standard-bearer and captured the enemy flag. Their victory had been swift.

Though the royalists suffered a defeat at San Lorenzo, it did not deter them from continuing their raids on the people in the area. But rather than continue an endless cycle of conflicts, San Martín tried a different approach—he invited Zabala to breakfast.

During each conflict with Zabala, San Martín had provided aid to his wounded soldiers and encouraged the people living in the area to keep peaceful relations with the royalists. San Martín led by example, refusing to take prisoners or demand ransoms. Through their discussions, San Martín convinced Zabala of the evils of the absolutism of the Spanish monarchy. Zabala felt that he could no longer defend it, and he defected to the revolutionaries and joined the forces under San Martín's command.

San Martín's popularity grew after that, but petty jealousies made him many enemies. After San Lorenzo, he was promoted to the commander of the forces protecting Buenos Aires, probably as much out of merit as it was to keep him from distinguishing himself further. San Martín knew exactly what was happening, and he was not happy babysitting Buenos Aires. He wanted an active command and demanded to be given one.

After Belgrano's defeat at Salta in 1813, San Martín got his opportunity. He was sent to replace the defeated general in the interior provinces. Both men had mutual respect and admiration for one another, so San Martín begged the government not to disgrace Belgrano when he took over for him, not wanting to add to Belgrano's pain.

What San Martín inherited from Belgrano was an army woefully undersupplied and unpaid. Their torn and worn-out clothing made them appear more like beggars than trained soldiers. San Martín had his work cut out for him.

He set out to rebuild and retrain the Army of the North. But the intense training his men received would go to waste in their position around Tucumán. San Martín knew that small skirmishes and their constant defensive position would not win—they needed to strike at the seat of the royalists in Lima.

But getting there would not be that simple. Enemies would try to stop him. He would need the support of friends in the government. He also knew that taking the route across the flat pampas would leave the army out in the open and an easy target. San Martín also did not want to leave Buenos Aires and Tucumán undefended. There would be much to do.

San Martín quietly schemed his way toward his goal of Lima. He recruited rough and tumble gauchos (South American cowboys) of the pampas to help defend Buenos Aires, telling them their call was in "defending their family and every Argentine family that was under the command of San Martin." He trained the men in the art of guerilla warfare, equipping them to defend their homes and cities. Once his plan progressed, he would leave them in the command of Martín de Güemes and two squadrons of well-trained veteran soldiers.

His next move would be to find a way to Lima. After considering all the options, he settled on the boldest and most difficult move— taking his army twelve thousand feet above sea level and over the

Andes Mountains. But to do that, he would need to find a way to leave Tucumán and move closer to his proposed route.

His aim was to get to Cuyo Province, but he could not just leave with the army and station himself wherever he wished. So, exaggerating an existing health problem, he wrote to authorities and said that his location in the lowlands was exacerbating his illness and that he wanted to go to Cuyo to recover. He requested the governorship of the province, and it was granted to him. Once there, he was stationed in the city of Mendoza, where he would be in the perfect position to carry out his plan.

He trained his soldiers for the journey; these became known as the Army of the Andes. San Martín plotted to link up with patriot forces in Chile once they made their journey over the mountains. From there, they would take ships to Peru, which was currently part of the United Provinces. First, his army would check their route to make sure it was clear, and on March 10th, 1816, they captured royalist scouts in the Action of Juncalito.

In 1817, San Martín was able to execute his plan of taking his army over the mountain range, earning him the nickname "Hannibal of the Andes." It would be the masterstroke in his contribution to South American liberation. On the other side of the Andes, he eventually met up with Simón Bolívar, and both men helped liberate Peru, Chile, and Bolivia from Spanish hands.

Chapter 11 – A Declaration of Independence

Back in Buenos Aires, the tide was turning. Although San Lorenzo had been a minor skirmish, it proved to be a great victory for the criollos, who, although outnumbered, proved to themselves that their tactical maneuvers could outmatch the Spanish.

It also bolstered confidence within the Triumvirate. In a government assembly session held shortly after the victory in San Lorenzo, they took measures that came just short of declaring independence. In 1814, King Ferdinand VII was returned to the throne of Spain, restoring absolutism and repealing the constitution drawn up in Buenos Aires. But now, riding high on their victory, the assembly decided that all mentions of the king of Spain be removed from important public documents and his likeness removed from coins. Titles of Spanish nobility were abolished, and the three symbols of the United Provinces were incorporated into the newly minted state seal and mentioned in the new national anthem.

But independence had still not yet been won. A series of confusing government changes followed, with the Second Triumvirate being replaced by the supreme director of the United Provinces of the Río de la Plata, the first of whom was Gervasio Antonio de Posadas. Just one year later, he was replaced by Carlos María de Alvear.

After only four months in office, a revolution ended Alvear's time in office, and he was replaced by Juan José Viamonte. Viamonte's stint as the supreme director was even shorter—just two days. His successor, José Rondeau, held office for only one day, with his absence causing him to be replaced shortly after being elected by the Constituting General Assembly. People called for a General Congress to be summoned, with delegates from all over the United Provinces of Río de la Plata.

Battles for independence also continued to rage. By early 1816, only the Río de la Plata region was still under the control of the revolutionaries. On March 24th, 1816, the Congress of Tucumán was finally inaugurated. Thirty-three deputies from the provinces made up the assembly, with it being agreed that the presidency of the assembly rotate between the members every month. Once in place, endless discussions and debates followed.

In early July of 1816, the congress could agree on one thing—their desire for independence. On July 9th, the votes were cast. Using the legal concept of retroversion of sovereignty to the people as a foundation, it was decided that Spain's control over the colony ended when King Ferdinand VII was deposed. They had long since taken care of their own affairs without the monarchy's aid or interference, and they no longer needed either.

The voting ended, and independence was officially declared. It was the end of an era, but the important choices that the congress needed to make were just beginning. Most immediate was the need to choose which form of government would be employed. Two different parties emerged. The Unitarian Party (*Unitarios*) favored a strong central government in which the provinces would enjoy no tax benefits derived from the port at Buenos Aires. The second party, the Federalists (*Federales*), preferred a weaker central government in which port taxes were distributed among the provinces. The debate would go on for several years, eventually plunging the new country into civil war.

Chapter 12 – The Wars Within

San Martín's epic journey into Chile and his victorious campaigns officially concluded Argentina's war for independence in 1818. Despite declaring independence in 1816, Spain was not going to concede, so the fight continued until the Argentine Army celebrated victories in Chile and Peru.

When the United Provinces of the Río de la Plata declared their independence, Juan Martín Pueyrredón was elected as its supreme director. His leadership gave the new country the stability it needed to finish the war against Spain. That stability would not last long, though.

The war against Spain ended, but the war within the country would begin. Unable to agree on how much power the central government should hold, the country became divided into numerous semi-autonomous states. Pueyrredón, for his part, wanted a stronger central government. Instead of support for his party, he faced rebellions from the provinces. In June of 1819, he resigned and moved an ocean away from the growing chaos, living in Europe for the next thirty years.

The enmity between the factions led to the formation of various political leagues, such as the League of the Free Peoples (also known as the Federal League) and the Unitarian League. Leaders were deposed and, in some instances, executed. Caudillos, local leaders similar to warlords, sprang up and held power over small areas. The two political parties, the Unitarians and the Federalists, each had their own leaders. The United Provinces were more divided than ever.

In 1826, a new constitution was drafted, and the country was declared a republic. Power would be shared between a president and the congress, but many were still dissatisfied. Seeing the move as a play for Buenos Aires to have more control over the provinces, rebellions continued, and civil warfare played out. Fighting continued between caudillos on both sides. Disunity threatened to cause Argentina to splinter into separate countries. The war became so consuming that trade and the economic welfare of the country suffered.

On December 1ˢᵗ, 1828, Buenos Aires was thrown into further turmoil by a coup. Juan Lavalle, a Unitarian, seized power from Governor Manuel Dorrego. It was a coup that would prove fatal for Dorrego. Twelve days after Lavalle overthrew Dorrego, he had Dorrego shot without trial. The violent overthrow angered many, even of his own party.

Bent on destroying the Federalist Party, Lavalle began his reign of terror. Other provinces refused to recognize Lavalle as a legitimate power. Caudillos and their militias rose up in rebellion. The situation became so chaotic that Lavalle turned to the one man he thought could regain control of the situation—José de San Martín.

Lavalle recognized that San Martín was a leader respected by both parties. He sent envoys to him in Montevideo and offered San Martín the command of the army in Buenos Aires Province. He was banking on San Martín's ability to restore peace to the interior provinces.

San Martín sensed the danger of the situation. The disturbed state of the country worried him greatly, and he perceived that an all-out civil war was imminent. He did not want to have to take sides, something he would surely be pressured to do. So, he refused the command and went into self-exile in Britain.

Without someone to quell the rising anger and dissension, Lavalle couldn't hold on to power for even a full year. In April of 1829, Juan Manuel de Rosas took his Federalist forces and went up against Lavalle in the Battle of Márquez Bridge. After his defeat, Lavalle was wounded by a gunshot and went into exile.[35]

After Rosas's victory against Lavalle, he took control of the government in Buenos Aires. At first, he ruled in partnership with Federalist governors of the provinces. But Rosas was not content with sharing, so the power of these rulers was systematically taken away, with Rosas beginning his road to becoming the supreme leader.[36]

---

[35] Some sources say he was accidentally shot by friendly fire, while others maintain he was assassinated by Federalists.

[36] Rosas's rise to power also saw the ascendency of cattle ranchers into the country's politics. It is noteworthy because they had had a dominant influence on the country's politics for over one hundred years.

Chapter 13 – The Rosas Regime Rises

Juan Manuel de Rosas abhorred democracy and liberal ideologies, and the constitutional idea of two parties was distasteful to him as well. He was a centralist and, as such, insisted on the supremacy of Buenos Aires. With a large portion of the population illiterate, Rosas believed they were unable to make proper decisions about elected representatives. Farcical rigged elections of politicians were set up, as Rosas believed it was the only way to create national stability. After dissolving the congress, he consolidated his power, with no official political body to challenge him. Though he was close to having absolute power and strived toward that goal, it would elude him for the time being.

In 1832, Rosas's term ended. Although he left office, the country would not see the end of Rosas or his ilk. With a new governor in office, Rosas remained busy gathering support for himself. He forcefully took lands from the native people in order to give them to supporters, cementing their allegiance. His removal of the "savages" from Argentinian lands had a positive effect on his reputation, with people hailing him as a brave defender of their fatherland. He became known as the "Restorer of Laws."

While Rosas was out conquering territories, his wife, María de la Encarnación Ezcurra (better known as simply Encarnación Ezcurra), was in Buenos Aires stirring up trouble. Knowing that the current governor, Juan Balcarce, would act against her husband at some point, it was no real surprise when his trial was announced. She quickly moved into action, setting up the stage for a coup against Balcarce.

Encarnación created a security force (akin to a secret police organization) called the Sociedad Popular Restauradora ("Popular Restorer Society"). It came to be known by the people as the Mazorca.[37] This force was sent to find and attack opposers and those conspiring against her husband, most of whom were Unitarians. Some of the enemies that fell by the Mazorca were real, but like the Reign of Terror during the French Revolution, many who fell were innocents imagined to be enemies.

Having a good relationship with many of the caudillos, Encarnación called on them to aid her husband. Riding across the pampas, they arrived in Buenos Aires. This led to what is known as the Revolution of the Restorers.

Leading a demonstration of Rosas's supporters in the city, the Restorers, as they called themselves, created a great commotion that shut down the city and prevented Balcarce's trial from taking place. Two generals sent to quash the disturbance ended up joining the rebel demonstration instead.

The Restorers blockaded the city so that no food, supplies, or livestock could come in. They took over the city's arsenals as well, leaving the government with no military backing.

As negotiations between the governor and the Restorers dragged on, food in the city became scarce. Balcarce and the city legislature were forced to act since new hostilities and famine threatened the city. Finally, the decision was made to remove Balcarce and appoint Juan

---

[37] Mazorca is thought to be a variation of the Spanish *mas horca*, meaning more hangings.

José Viamonte as governor. Balcarce and his ministers fled the city with a portion of the military.

Rosas's quest for absolute power got its second chance in 1835. After the assassination of La Rioja caudillo Juan Quiroga,[38] he was invited back to Buenos Aires for a five-year term as governor. The alleged "vote" that took place was another in a series of rigged elections—Rosas won the vote with a 99 percent majority. Once in control, he again demanded absolute power, this time holding a farce of a vote to ratify the constitution giving him the legal right to do so. His reign of terror would begin.

Rosas demanded complete loyalty, causing Unitarians to hide their political leanings, especially in public. People even went as far as to avoid wearing white- or blue-colored clothing or ribbons for fear they would be identified with the Unitarian Party and punished.

Men were required to have what was considered a "Federalist look"—a mustache and long sideburns. Those who could not or did not want to grow a mustache used fake ones in public in order to conform.

Even those living outside the city in the rural territories were not outside Rosas's grasp. He gathered many of the rugged, wild-living gauchos, whom he loved to imitate, and tamed them into serving involuntary labor or the militia.

Vocal political opponents could look forward to prison, exile, or execution. Describing the tyranny that reigned over Buenos Aires, eyewitness Anthony King wrote about the city's central marketplace where hangings took place. He said, "It was in the marketplace that Rosas hung the bodies of his many victims; sometimes decorating them in mockery, with ribands of the unitarian blue and even

---

[38] It is possible Rosas ordered the assassination himself. When later asked about it, he replied, "They say I ordered the assassination of the illustrious General Quiroga. But have they proved it?"

attaching to the corpses, labels, on which were inscribed the revolting words 'Beef with the hide.'"

Freedom of political ideologies was not the only thing suppressed under Rosas's iron fist. Freedom of the press became nonexistent, and newspapers expressing opposition views were burned in public squares. School curriculums were changed, and only certain books were allowed. Teachers were compelled to teach only the values promoted by Rosas's conservative party and sing his praises, indoctrinating their students with party propaganda. Portraits of Rosas were put upon church altars, a fitting symbol of the worship he was ostensibly demanding. He had created a cult of personality around himself.

United States diplomat William A. Harris wrote a chilling description of what life was like under Rosas's regime. "Such is the terror—the crushing fear—which is inspired by one man over that multitude, which now submits to his decrees with a zeal, apparently as ardent, as it is certainly abject and submissive. There is not a complaint heard. The calm and dark waters of despotism are never disturbed by the slightest ripple. Not a breath of free thought or manly speech passes over them, but they lie dead and deep, into which every vestige of the people's liberty and freedom has sunk and disappeared. Yet Gen'l. [General] Rosas is the only man who could keep them together for twenty-four hours; and this he does by the extraordinary energy of his character, and the unqualified fear with which he has inspired them."

As was inevitable, there were those who dared to oppose Rosas, including some of the top intellectuals in the country. Secret revolutionary organizations arose, among them Joven Argentina (Young Argentina).[39] Rebellions from within the government appeared and were suppressed, with conspiring politicians and military leaders caught and exiled or executed.

---

[39] Also known as the Asociación de Mayo.

Even Juan Lavalle returned out of exile for a short period, leading an army as a general in a failed movement in Buenos Aires in the fall of 1839. Other rebellions rose up and failed, but after almost two decades, enthusiasm for Rosas's rule had waned. Tired of the reign of terror, popular support of his government within Buenos Aires Province declined until it became just about nonexistent. Exiles dreamed of returning to oust him from office. The wealthy commercial cattle ranchers (*estancieros*), who had heartily supported Rosas, were now soured by his heavy taxation and conscriptions. Their own power had waned, with their numbers being replaced by sheep farmers who were not committed to backing Rosas politically or through militias. But it was a dispute with Montevideo that would lead to Rosas's ultimate downfall.

In early February 1852, a military leader rose up who would finally be able to defeat Rosas. Justo José de Urquiza, the governor of Entre Ríos, formed alliances with lesser provincial leaders. Angered by Rosas's blockade preventing trade with Montevideo—trade that many provinces relied upon—Urquiza began preparations for a rebellion.

When he believed the time was right, he put out a statement, calling for Rosas to resign. But knowing Rosas would not go quietly, Urquiza gathered ten thousand cavalry troops and planned his next move.

On February 3ʳᵈ, Urquiza and his allies struck. They positioned their troops at Monte Caseros. Rosas did not take the threat as seriously as he should have. Poor management caused his military commander to quit, and morale fell. Desertions rose.

But it wasn't just Rosas's military that was saddled with problems. The bulk of Urquiza's forces were not professional soldiers—they were ill-disciplined gauchos. But even the professional ranks experienced daunting issues. Among their forces were men within the Aquino Regiment, men who were loyal to Rosas. They mutinied, killing their captain and going over to join Rosas's army.

The command of Urquiza's forces was also disunified. Instead of leading his allied forces as one army, he allowed each commander to fight as they saw fit.

Despite having no skill or experience as a military commander, Rosas decided to lead the charge into battle himself. But first, he would sit and wait for Urquiza and his allies to come to him.

When the battle began, Urquiza recklessly led his charge. After just a few hours, Rosas's army began to run out of ammunition, causing the flanks to collapse. One commander ordered the men to find and use ammunition dropped on the battlefield, but in the end, it was futile. With no ammo, the professional regiments were able to quickly overrun Rosas's forces.

After six hours of fighting, the battle ended, with 1,500 of Rosas's forces dead and 7,000 captured as prisoners of war. What became of Rosas himself, though? He was shot through the hand during the battle. Abandoned by his most trusted men, Rosas fled the battlefield defeated and alone. Boarding a ship in the night, he sailed to England, where he died in exile.

Rosas's rule had lasted for more than twenty years. However, despite his success in Buenos Aires Province and his ambitions of ruling all of Argentina, the thirteen other provinces of the United Provinces of the Río de la Plata maintained their own independent governance. By the end of his dictatorship, he had neither helped his own province nor Argentina as a whole. In fact, he left Buenos Aires isolated from other provinces that had refused to come under Rosas's "Argentina."

Chapter 14 – Rise of a Republic

Immediately following the Battle of Caseros and Rosas's flight from the country, Urquiza took over national affairs. In August of 1853, delegates from the provinces met to sign the San Nicolás Agreement, making Urquiza the provisional director of the Argentine Confederation, which was established in 1831.

Of course, Urquiza would face stiff opposition. The wealthy and elite of Buenos Aires did not appreciate his restrictions on their control over the port city. They felt that Urquiza had the makings of a despot who jeopardized their rights. Urquiza would have to find a way to quell their anger so as not to face more violent uprisings. He would let the constitution do that work. He assigned two men to draft wording that would ease the harshness of the restrictions and be friendlier to porteño interests.[40]

Urquiza called together governors and delegates to a constitutional congress that September. His directorship had ended, and he went to meet the congressional delegates in Santa Fe. They were going to revisit the previously failed constitutions of 1819 and 1826, but this time, they would make reforms modeled after the Constitution of the

---

[40] A porteño or "port person" was used to refer to a citizen of Buenos Aires.

United States. Inspired by the United States Constitutional Congress in Philadelphia, each province was to send two delegates to the assembly in an attempt to ensure equal representation.[41]

Only three days after Urquiza got to Santa Fe, things began to fall apart again. Revolts ensued, and Buenos Aires Province recalled their delegates from the assembly. They called on the other provinces to do the same. When the other provinces refused, Buenos Aires sent forces to attack the other provinces in an attempt to weaken Urquiza's power. Their forces were repelled with nothing having been gained—the other provinces joined the constitutional convention, which began its sessions without representation from Buenos Aires.

Consultations with the United States Constitution, redactions, negotiations, and revisions went on for weeks. For some, the freedom of religion was a problematic issue, and the representatives firmly opposed it, worried that the existence of cults could cause new caudillos to rise and stir up trouble against the government. An attempt was made to mandate that everyone profess the Catholic religion, including the native peoples. In the end, individual religious freedoms remained intact, with only the president obligated to profess Catholicism.

The matter of Buenos Aires was also discussed. Many favored ending the monopoly held by the elite porteños, wanting to federalize the city in order to separate it from governance by the province. This would be sure to anger the porteños. Doing it would practically ensure that Buenos Aires would never rejoin the confederation. Difficult negotiations ended in a compromise—Buenos Aires would be the capital city with certain stipulations and room for modifications within the law should it need to be changed in the future.

---

[41] Some historians argue that the representation was not exactly equal. Delegates with widely varying backgrounds, educations, and interests were sent, causing discrepancies among the delegates. Not all the delegates were popular among the people they represented either, with some of them having spent many years away in exile during Rosas's rule.

The assembly also drew up articles for a republic government system with three independent branches: legislative, judicial, and executive. Provincial governments would retain some powers according to their own constitutions.

A congress and senate would be created, with representatives from each province and the city of Buenos Aires having a lower house called the Chamber of Deputies to directly represent the people. A national supreme court composed of nine judges and two prosecutors was also formed, with it being decided for it to sit in the capital city.

In May of 1853, the hard work of drafting and revising was concluded. The final draft was approved by the provinces (all except for Buenos Aires). It was considered to be an important step in unifying the country and laid the foundation for the government going forward.

Chapter 15 – A Controversial Campaign Ushers in the "Golden Years"

After the War of the Triple Alliance, a disastrous war for Paraguay that pitted them against Argentina, Brazil, and Uruguay, Argentina saw additional changes in the consolidation of power, its military, and development of infrastructure. In 1862, Buenos Aires Province rejoined the rest of the provinces, uniting the country. Thus began a period of political stability, a relief from all the turmoil of the previous seventy years.

By 1880, Buenos Aires began its "golden years," and the economy boomed, giving rise to a middle class comprised of artisans, merchants, farmers, government employees, businessmen, and others. Telephone lines and railroads were built, connecting the provinces to each other and the surrounding nations. Public education flourished, allowing illiteracy to drop. The advent of steamships led to faster trade and travel, including the more efficient transport of meat. During this time, many books were published, newspapers were founded, and even a world-class opera house was built in Buenos Aires. It was becoming a city that could rival any in Europe.

The decade before those "golden years" saw a government that encouraged immigration from Europe, particularly Welsh settlers, to the remote Patagonia valleys. However, the attempt at Europeanizing the population was not without pitfalls, as many of the natives still lived on open or unowned lands. Wanting these frontier lands to further entice European immigration, a campaign began that would become one of the most controversial episodes in the country's history.

In 1875, the first proposed plan would populate the desert regions with landowning immigrants but leave the native populations intact. But shortly after, the peace treaty signed with the government was broken by two native chieftains when they brought 3,500 warriors against several towns and cities. The attack resulted in 700 settlers being either killed or captured and a loss of 300,000 cattle. It was not an isolated incident. Similar raids continued until both sides came to terms. In some instances, natives signed treaties with settlers and assimilated into life within their forts. Some tribes allied with the government, even fighting for the army of Argentina, while others remained neutral. The arrangement settled matters until 1877 when Minister of War Adolfo Alsina died. General Julio Argentino Roca stepped in, and the strategy changed completely, beginning the Conquest of the Desert, a military campaign.

Rather than one of peaceful coexistence, Roca felt that the native population was a threat. Cities were being attacked, white settlers were being killed, and their cattle were being taken by the native tribes. Many of the tribal warriors were, by this time, able to fight with the most modern of weapons, with some attacks against the Argentine Army carried out with Winchesters and British Martini-Henry rifles. Not content with peace treaties that could be broken at any time, Roca felt that the country needed to rid itself of the native threat by subduing, annihilating, or driving out the people. The course would now change from one of "merciful civilization" to one of "offensive warfare."[42]

He began a campaign of systematic attacks against tribal settlements. Numerous violent conflicts took place, and by December 1878, four hundred natives had been killed and four thousand captured. Roca's forces also managed to acquire 150 settlers who had been captured and 15,000 heads of cattle that had been previously taken. Some eyewitness accounts told of horrors committed by Roca's army, including mass executions and the killing of prisoners.

The Mapuche tribe of the Patagonia region had been the only people to remain unconquered by the Spanish during the colonial era. However, Roca's campaign saw one thousand Mapuche killed and fifteen thousand displaced from their lands.

In 1880, Roca was elected president, but he hadn't finished his campaign. He appointed Colonel Conrado Villegas to continue the conquest and commanded the resistance to continue pushing south.

In the final battle, on October 18th, 1884, three thousand native warriors under the command of Chiefs Foyel and Inacayal surrendered after two months of fighting. They were the last holdouts, and their surrender ended the campaign.

Despite the controversial war with the native tribes, the country continued to prosper. Roca and the "Generation of 80" (a group of powerful landowning politicians) ushered in the stability the country needed to accelerate its economic growth.

---

[42] Many contemporary writers of the time spoke of this action as genocide. Many in modern times have agreed with this assessment, while others have hailed Roca as a hero and savior who helped stop and prevent further violent actions by the native people.

But as Argentina continued to prosper and grow, as immigrants from new countries came in with their own ways and cultures, and as old traditions began to wane and give way to more modern living, a crisis of national identity arose. What really was the heart of Argentina?

Chapter 16 – A Crisis of Cultural Identity

As if coming into its adulthood, Argentina's new growth touched off a need for a "national identity." Mass immigration and modernization had changed the character of portions of the country, bringing with it a cosmopolitan influence that had been preferred and nurtured by Buenos Aires. As it neared the turn of the 20th century, Buenos Aires had become the noisiest and brashest city in Latin America.

Author Thomas Turner, who lived in Argentina from 1885 to 1890, wrote about the impression of friends who came to the capital city with preconceived notions of finding it wild and uncivilized. He was amused that they arrived, as he said, "so thoroughly imbued with these silly notions that the outfits they have brought with them would have been better suited to the necessities of the Australian bush or the Canadian backwoods than to the requirements of life they were likely to experience in Argentina. Where they should have brought dress suits and dancing shoes, they came provided with a whole defensive arsenal and a supply of coarse apparel."

During the early 1900s, minister G. L Morrill also wrote about Buenos Aires and the cosmopolitan air it had about it. He compared the city to Paris, finding the city's "architecture, fashionable stores, cafes, and sidewalks filled with little tables where males and females flirt and gossip." He also commented on the newspaper kiosks and girls selling flowers on the corners. He mentioned that the "side streets are crowded with cars and carts and the main avenues with taxis which rest in the center or rush up and down either side." The center of the city was also compared to New York's Broadway; he called it "the big white way" that at night shone with "electric lights blazing a trail to the cafes and theaters."

Many in the cities balked in contempt for what was seen as the "uncivilized" influence of the rough-riding gauchos, who wore their baggy bombachas and lived by their saddles, and the cattle ranch societies of the interior frontiers. Though the gauchos spent their days on the pampas hunting and herding cattle, their legacy and imprint on Argentine culture go far beyond that.

In fact, those colorful horsemen greatly influenced the country's culture, becoming somewhat legendary, with folk heroes finding life in ballads and epic tales. While older ballads were written in the Spanish romance style and focused on passion, gallantry, heartbreak, and tragedy, the more modern gaucho works took a different tone. As the country changed, many pieces of gaucho literature (such as the famous poem *El Gaucho Martín Fierro*) focused on the struggle between their traditional life and modern society. But as a whole, the gauchos' writings gave artistic and also very real glimpses into their life and culture, a culture that could be seen woven into society even as the days of the traditional gaucho waned.

Though the role of the gaucho changed over time—by the late 1800s, many of them worked as ranch hands instead of free-riding wranglers—they had gained a reputation for being the strong silent type (similar to the cowboys of the United States). They were also known to have a violent bent when provoked, but this trait proved crucial as they helped fight for the country's independence. Their knowledge of often remote and rugged terrains, along with their contribution to the war of independence from Spain, raised them to hero status. They became a national symbol for Argentina, leading to a romanticization of their culture and lifestyle.

Despite their wild reputation, the gauchos and those living in the countryside were especially noted for their hospitality. Colonel J. Anthony King expressed his appreciation for this quality when he wrote that "whether in health or sickness, the traveler is always welcome to their houses and boards." Naturalist Charles Darwin, who also spent time in Argentina, was struck by the manners of the gauchos. He even said that they were "very superior to those who reside in the towns. The gaucho is invariably the most obliging, polite, and hospitable. I did not meet with even one instance of rudeness or inhospitality."

Darwin was also awed by the skills the gauchos possessed when it came to horses. He told an entertaining story of an episode he once witnessed. He talked about a time he was "amused by the dexterity with which a gaucho forced a...horse to swim a river." He said the gaucho next "stripped off his clothes and jumping on its back rode into the river till it was out of its depth." The gaucho then slipped off the back of the horse and grabbed its tail. Every time the horse turned around, the gaucho splashed water in its face to keep it moving forward. Darwin next related, "As soon as the horse touched bottom on the other side, the man pulled himself on, and was firmly seated, bridle in hand, before the horse gained the bank. A naked man on a naked horse is a fine spectacle; I had no idea how well the two animals suited each other."

Even though the gauchos and country folk were friendly and kind, the rugged interior of the country was not without its perils. Frances Bond Head, an English miner who spent two years in the country, wrote about the dangers he faced riding across the pampas during this time period. He said that when doing so, it was "absolutely necessary to be armed, as there are many robbers or *saltadors*, particularly in the desolate province of Santa Fe." In order to avoid trouble, he said that he "always rode badly dressed...that although I once passed through them with no one but a child as a postilion, they thought it not worth their while to attack me." He also mentioned the necessity of traveling well-armed, always having "carried two braces of detonating pistols in a belt, and a short detonating double-barreled gun in my hand." Head went on to tell that he had one rule for himself—"never to be an instant without [his] arms, and to cock both barrels of my gun whenever I met any gauchos."

Head also spoke about the dangers from native peoples on the pampas, likening riding through their territories as going through a "gauntlet." But by the time the "golden years" began in the late 1800s, seeing free Native Americans was somewhat of a novelty to Europeans. This is highlighted by Lady Florence Dixie when she wrote in her book, *Across Patagonia*, "We had not gone far when we saw a rider coming slowly towards us, and in a few minutes we found ourselves in the presence of a real Patagonia [native]. We reined in our horses when he got close to us, to have a good look at him, and he doing the same."

Other European adventurers, such as Julius Beerbohm, had positive impressions of the indigenous people they met in Patagonia, with Beerbohm saying they were intelligent, gentle, and their "conscientious behavior in their social and domestic relations" were "superior" to "the general run of civilized white men."

By the time Argentina's "golden years" had ended, many influences on the country's culture could be seen. But some liberals, such as writer Ricardo Rojas, argued that the root of Argentina's identity lay with the native people and a love of the natural land. Although many of the original native cultures have been lost over time, it can still be seen in some of their traditional clothing, music, food, local customs, beliefs, and even speech styles.

Though its hodgepodge of cultural influences may have given the country something of an identity crisis, the rapidly modernizing country was about to experience a crisis greater than that of deciding its identity.

Chapter 17 – Worker Strikes Descend into Anarchy

The workers had taken to the streets. Angry over falling wages, rising prices, and layoffs, they vigorously protested the lot of the common wage earner. The growing unrest was becoming a thorn in the government's side. The country was already dealing with the economic fallout caused by the world war raging in Europe. That economic crisis only served to incite more anger in the workers who were feeling the brunt of it.

La Federación Obrera Regional Argentina (FORA), which was formed in 1902 and in operation until 1909, rose up against anti-labor legislation. Headed by renowned anarchist Pietro Gori, strikes were organized to protest employers and the legislation that allowed businesses to foster unfair working conditions. The strikes may have started out relatively peaceful, but over the next few years, the protests would descend into something far more violent.

The organization led by an anarchist unsurprisingly bred anarchy. Bombs were planted on trains, theaters, and other public locations. Police cracked down, and workers became even more militant. Earlier bombs had targeted civilians, but the focus turned onto government agencies and authorities. Bombs exploded in the Spanish consulate in

Rosario; nineteen-year-old anarchist Simón Radowitzky, wielding a handheld bomb, killed Buenos Aires police chief Ramón Falcón and his secretary. The president himself was not exempt from the wrath of the workers. President José Alcorta, who was targeted in 1908, experienced a narrow escape from death when a bomb was hurled at his vehicle while he drove through Buenos Aires.

A large march in May 1909 was broken up by police. With twelve protesters dead and one hundred wounded, anarchists continued to ratchet their response with increasing levels of violence. A second presidential assassination attempt was made in July 1916, this time with a gun being wielded on President Victorino de la Plaza as he inspected military troops during an Independence Day celebration.

The violence continued into 1918. Strikes devolved into anarchists destroying train tracks and trains, burning carriages brimming with wheat. The Argentine military had to be called in to help with the situation.

Tensions persistently simmered, and in January 1919, they finally boiled over in a week that came to be known as Semana Trágica (Tragic Week). The trouble on January 4th, 1919, began at the Vasena metal works in the suburbs of Buenos Aires. It was an unremarkable strike at first, but the scene took a violent turn when picketers shot three policemen escorting loads of metal. One of those policemen would die of his injuries.

Three days later, on January 7th, police chief Elpidio González arrived at Vasena to negotiate with the labor union leaders. The striking workers had no patience for their talks. Before González even left his vehicle, the workers overturned it and set it on fire. They then turned on the army lieutenant who was escorting González and shot him dead. Police fought to get the situation back under control. The clash resulted in five workers being killed and twenty wounded.

Rather than quell the wrath of the militant workers, the killing of their fellow employees fostered violent revenge later that night. Groups of workers from Vasena and the bayside port hid inside houses, waiting in ambush. They targeted army officers, attacking and killing a number of them in the streets. In the chaos, an innocent civilian also paid with his life—he was in the wrong place at the wrong time.

That same night, demonstrations were heating up across Buenos Aires. Police became trapped on rooftops, surrounded by a mob that had become completely out of control. Army riflemen had to be sent to their rescue. Not even civilian rescue workers were safe that night. Ambulance drivers and paramedics tending to those killed and wounded in the violence were compelled to carry weapons in order to defend themselves.

As dawn broke on January 8th, the situation at the Vasena factory had become critical. Thousands had gathered, intent on burning the building to the ground. They did not care that their four hundred fellow workers who refused to take part in the violence were trapped inside. An army regiment was deployed to stop them from committing mass murder by arson.

On January 9th, funerals commenced for the five protesters killed by police two days earlier. Armed mourners followed funeral wagons through the streets. Their anger boiled over, and they destroyed property and burned vehicles along the route.

After reaching the tram station, the funeral procession took their rage out on train cars, breaking every window, glass raining down inside and out. A group broke off, a church in their crosshairs. They burned the church before moving on to a store. There, police caught up with them. The police fired into the procession; numerous people were struck by bullets and lay in the street dead or wounded.

A citywide rampage touched off. In the midafternoon, thousands stormed the tram station. Congressmen of the lower Chamber of Deputies became increasingly frustrated. But rather than take action to quell the violence, they turned on each other, throwing notebooks at other members who angered them.

Meanwhile, the situation at Vasena continued to rage. The angry mob barricaded the doors with cargo wagons, blocking off any escape for those inside. Then they set the entrance on fire. After seventeen hours, as another day dawned, the mob outside tried to gain access to the factory. Once inside, they planned to seize and murder the British company directors they were besieging. With the lives of the managers in imminent peril, an urgent call to President Hipólito Yrigoyen went out. He gave one order to the military and police—shoot to kill.

The order served to only worsen the situation. The number of dead and wounded quickly mounted. And instead of dispersing the raging protesters, the violence incited them to become ever more destructive.

The British companies in control of the subway and tram stations refused to stop service, despite the strike. After only an hour and a half, enraged strikers stopped two train lines and hijacked several cars, setting them on fire.

Continued police action against the striking workers called for a discussion among the members of FORA. They met that night and decided on a twenty-four-hour citywide strike throughout Buenos Aires. It would not serve to ease tensions on any front.

Over the next few days, three army divisions were sent by the federal government to help defend the city. Within hours, a call went back to the president: "The troops are insufficient." Three branches of the military were sent for reinforcements. Infantry, cavalry, and artillery divisions positioned themselves strategically around the city.

Even the police needed the assistance of the military. Thousands of angry strikers had descended on police stations around the city, including the city's police headquarters. They weren't just looking to storm the buildings; they went with the aim of seizing police arsenals for themselves. At least two officers died as they defended their stations to their literal deaths.

Violence continued to break out against the troops sent to control the situation. But it was their weapons arsenals that tempted rioters to emboldened action. On January 10th, under the dark of night, thirty armed men attempted to loot the Campo de Mayo army barracks. Their brazen attack was met with a rifle platoon that forced them to retreat.

Citizen vigilante groups formed, ostensibly to back up the police force. The presence of one group, in particular, the Argentine Patriotic League, touched off a spate of violence against the Jewish and Russian population in the city. They were dragged from their homes and beaten, with a mounting number being shot and killed.

The fierce fighting effectually paralyzed the city. Stores, hotels, and bars shut their doors. Customs buildings at the port closed. No newspaper headlines greeted the porteños since there were no media to let them know what was happening. Telephone lines and other communication networks shut down, further cutting the people off.

Transportation came to a standstill. In a show of solidarity with the striking workers, the railroad union stopped train service across the country. With the port closed, food in the city began to run out, and what food remained jumped in price over the course of a day.

On January 11th, chaos spread to the outlying suburbs. Protesters in Barracas attempted to overtake the local police department. Firemen with rifles arrived on the scene, backed up by an army regiment. A four-hour gun battle ensued, eventually forcing the rioters to retreat but not until several had been shot dead in the fray.

The city had been turned into a virtual war zone. Burned-out cars, trams, and other materials were turned into barricades. The city sawmill and grain wagons were set ablaze and burned. Bullets rained down from windows and rooftops, ambushing police and military troops in the streets. Emergency workers and innocent civilians were not always able to dodge trouble, some becoming casualties of the battle.

The chaos became a perfect cover for other groups to rise up with their own agendas. The authorities in Buenos Aires got a call from the Montevideo police force that a communist plot was brewing and that it was aimed at seizing both capital cities. Members of the "First Soviet of the Federal Republic of Argentine Soviets" were raided and arrested. Elsewhere in the city, the youth of the Patriotic League mobilized, stating, "we cannot passively observe the events that alter the social order," despite "the divergences that separate us from the government." Employers had also resorted to hiring right-wing "death squads" to subdue striking workers.

President Yrigoyen decided that drastic measures needed to be taken. He declared martial law in the city. The government sent General Luis Dellepiane and over one thousand reinforcements from various branches of the military in hopes that the chaotic scene could finally be subdued. The strong military presence had a desirable effect, causing disturbances to subside.

In total, thirty thousand police and soldiers took part in the fight. By the time the week finished, as many as 1,500 civilians, police, and troops had died, with hundreds injured and thousands arrested.[43]

However, not all were done with their work. On January 13th, anarchists set out to make another attempt, this time trying to seize the weapons arsenal of a local police station. A naval cruiser put them

---

[43] The numbers of arrested vary widely from over 3,500 to 55,000. The number of dead and injured widely varied as well. Media reporting was apparently skewed based on political leanings or affiliations.

under heavy fire, forcing them to retreat. The total anarchy of the Semana Trágica died down, and although the anarchists' work in the country would not be finished for some years, it would experience a sharp decline.

Despite the violent strikes and protests of that week, Argentina's economy continued to prosper, and its golden era continued. But a major crash loomed on the horizon.

Chapter 18 – The Great Depression and the World at War

On the eve of World War I, Argentina had been prospering, and its future looked bright. The booming growth experienced during its golden era, largely due to it being a leading world exporter of meat, corn, and flax, allowed the country to be ranked among the top ten wealthiest countries in the world.

The shine of the golden era was dulled in 1930 when the Great Depression crashed down on the world. Though the Great Depression hadn't impacted Argentina the same way that it had other developed nations, there was considerable damage due to the fallout from the crash of other nations' economies. Argentina relied heavily on exports, and foreign trade was now reduced due to the economic chaos experienced by its trade allies. Demand from Europe and the United States dried up as if overnight. Argentina's ranking among the wealthiest countries began to slide.

The fallout created a domino effect. Reliance on exports had meant customs revenues for the government. As these dried up, so did pay to public workers. The money was no longer there, and the government had a hard time paying employees. Worker unrests again simmered.

Farmers and countryside workers from ranches also faced an economic downturn. Lack of demand for their products, as well as the lack of needed imports to sustain their businesses, meant they were no longer able to sustain themselves. Millions relocated from rural areas to larger cities and their outskirts. Joblessness and their poor economic condition meant they could hardly afford housing in the city areas, and the first shanty towns (*villas miseria*) in the country sprang up. Those who migrated from the country to the city also lacked political knowledge or sophistication, something that would heavily impact the country in the coming decades.

Turmoil within the government fostered more instability. Election fraud, persecution of political opponents, and government corruption diverted attention from the economic crisis. It set the stage for the next big political upset—the September Revolution.

On September 5th, 1930, General José Félix Uriburu led a small group of soldiers into Buenos Aires. They faced little opposition as they marched toward the presidential mansion, Casa Rosada. Uriburu and his forces toppled the government and seized control. They justified their actions, saying the coup was simply a response to popular demand. The large crowds of supporters throughout the city held up that argument, cheering the military procession as they passed.

Major changes to Argentina's political landscape followed. The constitution founded in 1853 was suspended, paving the way for Uriburu to mold the government structure to his liking. He banned political parties, suspended democratic elections, and proposed a new government based on a mix of fascism and corporatism. The Infamous Decade had now begun.

On the heels of the Great Depression and Uriburu's coup, the country was in a tough economic situation. Numerous reforms, some controversial, were instituted to help Argentina become self-sufficient through industry and agriculture. Trade agreements were signed with Great Britain, and high tariffs on imported goods were imposed, minimizing competition from foreign trade and forcing the people to buy domestic products.

Though the focus on industrial products, like textiles, leather, and home appliances, caused agriculture to take a backseat, the growth of new crops, like oilseed, soybeans, sugarcane, cotton, and others, helped Argentina stay on top as one of the world's leading agricultural producers.

As the rest of the world plunged into the chaos of World War II, Argentina was experiencing an economic upturn. Trade with Great Britain and self-sufficiency began to restore the country's economic state.

Despite its massive population of German and Italian immigrants, President Roberto María Ortiz announced the "prudent neutrality" of Argentina at the start of World War II in 1939. The heavy influence of the German population and Allied and Axis pressures made that neutrality difficult at times, but the official position of the country never changed. Argentina wanted to keep good relationships, especially in regards to trade, with European countries. The country's neutral stance during the First World War had also been very popular. With Argentina's economy on the upswing toward recovery, neutrality in the war remained important to its stability and continued growth. The war, though, sharply divided the country.

In September 1941, as the Nazis laid siege to Stalingrad and Britain suffered under the explosions of Axis bombings, an Argentine naval officer, Captain Ernesto Villanueva, was planning for a different military operation, wholly separate from the world war that was raging elsewhere.

Back in 1765, the British had captured and occupied a small archipelago in the South Atlantic. The *Islas Malvinas* (Falkland Islands) had long been under colonial control, but with the British entrenched in warfare half a world away, Villanueva saw it as the perfect opportunity to take them back.

Using only army and navy landing troops, he planned a surprise dawn action on Port Stanley. Protecting these troops would be the air-naval fleet, which helped destroy defensive batteries stationed in Uraine Bay. With battleships, cruisers, and over one thousand troops, the seizure of the island did not appear to have many difficulties. What they feared most, though, was what might come after.

There was a good chance that after World War II, Britain would turn its attention back to its seized colonial islands. More armed conflict was sure to ensue then. After reevaluating the situation, the military decided to abort the mission for the time being. It was not the end, though, as the fight for the Falkland Islands would simply be on hold, albeit for several decades.

As the United States was pulled into World War II, Argentina faced increasing pressure from the Allied forces to join. But it wasn't really military support that they were concerned about. Large German firms were operating in Argentina, which remained closely linked with Germany even during the war. Allied forces feared that they were supporting major Nazi espionage operations, with Argentina being used as their base for Latin America.

The United States Army's "Blue Book" saw great potential for a resurgence of Nazism in the country. They already saw the influence, such as interference with Argentina's elections, subsidization of the press, which led to widespread media propaganda, and the shipment of strategic materials necessary to the German war effort in Europe.

After World War II, the Nazi threat was minimized, but there remained a different type of Nazi threat. Fleeing the wrath of the Allies, many top-ranking Nazi officials knew they would not be able to hide in Europe. Hoping to blend in with the existing German population, many turned to Argentina.

Although Argentina did not invite or specifically welcome Nazi criminals, some maintain that the government did not pursue them as vigorously as it should have. Jewish organizations accused the country of being complicit with refugee Nazi leaders, allowing the country to be a safe haven to two of the most notable war criminals of the century—Adolf Eichmann and Josef Mengele.[44,45]

The world war had now drawn to a close, and Argentina's economy was continuing to improve. However, the backbone of that economy, the working class, remained discontent with their wages and working conditions. It paved the way for someone who they felt would champion their cause—Juan Perón.

---

[44] Eichmann had been captured by US troops but was able to escape before facing trial for war crimes in Nuremberg. Using a fake identity, he was able to travel through numerous countries before making it to Argentina in 1950. He was eventually caught in the early 1960s through a secret operation led by Israeli Mossad agents. He was returned to Israel for trial, where he was convicted and hanged for his part in the atrocities committed in Nazi concentration camps.

[45] Mengele became known as the "Angel of Death" due to the horrific medical experiments he performed on Auschwitz concentration camp prisoners. He was never captured, but in 1979, he drowned off the coast of Brazil.

Chapter 19 – The Perón Era Begins

After the military overthrew the government in the Revolution of 1943, a young army colonel named Juan Perón was appointed as the national secretary of labor and social welfare. During his tenure, he increased wages, pensions, and benefits for workers. Factory employees would now also receive paid vacations. Labor unions set up to support workers' rights saw an unprecedented gain in power.

Previous governments had ignored the complaints of the laborers, at times suppressing their protests with violence as they had earlier in the century. Perón saw the potential strength of the working class, knowing there was an opportunity there that he could capitalize on. His reforms in favor of the common worker not only won him large support but also won him the election for the presidency in 1946.

Before he won the presidency, however, Perón had been arrested and imprisoned by his opponents within the very government for which he worked. His opponents, seeing the popularity and support he enjoyed among the hundreds of thousands of mostly unskilled unionized workers that had moved from the rural areas, feared they would want to put Perón in power. And they feared that Perón would try to grab it.

Several days after his arrest, between 250,000 and 350,000 supporters gathered outside of Casa Rosada. The imposing crowd shouted in demand of Perón's release. At 11 p.m., the man they called for stepped out onto the balcony and addressed the gathered people. Dramatically taking on the role of a caudillo, his address to the crowd, according to one writer, was full of "quasi-religious mystic overtones."

His charismatic speech stirred the people. So, when Perón ran for president in 1946, he won by a landslide. He got to work immediately.

Using the corporatist model, Perón created a state monopoly that controlled Argentina's most heavily exported goods. However, his policies continued to work in favor of the laborers, increasing their benefits and even encouraging them to strike, having created a system that would help settle affairs in their favor.

Perón's goal was to remove the workers' ability to act autonomously, but the working class loved his policies so much that there was no opposition in his path to achieving them. Over a four-year period, workers' wages went up 25 percent. Perón nationalized British railways and other utilities, a move that won him adoration from numerous groups. In 1947, he was able to declare Argentina economically independent, having paid off all its foreign debts.

His second wife, Eva (popularly called Evita), a former model and actress, was also a popular figure that gained him support. Since she was much younger than her husband, she was easily shaped under his political tutelage. Not content to sit on the sidelines, she became an asset to her husband, who came to rely on her heavily. She gave fiery impassioned speeches supporting her husband, met with many dignitaries and heads of state, and helped organize a labor movement. She championed women's rights, helping them to win the right to vote. Coming from a humble background herself, she was sympathetic to the disadvantaged, creating charitable organizations to help the less fortunate. She won the affection and adoration of the people.

However, outside of Argentina, she was not as warmly regarded. In Britain, King George VI refused her request for a state visit, even though his Foreign Office advisers pressed for it. She ended up canceling her trip, citing exhaustion as her reason for not going. However, she regarded their move as a snub.

The situation was even worse during her visit to Switzerland. Far from just a royal snub, people in the streets threw stones through the windshield of the car she traveled in. Though uninjured, her pride certainly took another hit as protesters threw tomatoes at her while she sat with the foreign minister. Though the tomatoes missed her, they did not miss the foreign minister, and Eva's dress suffered from the resulting splatter. Having had enough of European "hospitality," she returned to Argentina.

In late 1949, during Perón's first term, Eva started to exhibit signs of severe illness. She began to complain of severe abdominal pain and weakness, something that lasted several months. Then, on January 9th, 1950, she fainted while in public. The diagnosis was grim—she was in the advanced stages of cervical cancer. She did not want the public or her husband to find out. In order to excuse her hospital stay, it was reported that she had an appendectomy.

The fainting spells and extreme weakness continued over the next year. It was nearly impossible to hide her ill health. Despite this, her husband, still unaware of just how poor her diagnosis was, tried to have her installed as the vice president of the new Peronist Party. Eva knew it was not practical, but she did not have to disclose her health reason, as her bid was unequivocally denied by the military and upper-class elites.

But Perón had bigger issues than the failed bid. His economic policies were popular with the people, but they soon ran him into trouble. He had inadvertently discouraged the growth of agricultural exports, a mainstay of the country's economy. Government spending on programs such as transportation, worker housing, and public works drained the coffers. Perón was forced to borrow enormous sums of money in order to keep them running.

Inflation rose rapidly, and wages plunged. Wanting to fix the economy quickly, he put strict limits on wages and prices, then tightened restrictions on government spending. He began to take more power, making decisions without consulting other officials within his government. He started censoring newspapers. His popularity slipped further and further.

Though the country was nearly bankrupt and he had incurred the anger of just about everyone across the board—newspapers, middle-class businesses, poor farmers, wealthy landowners, even the industrial workers who had propelled him to power—he changed the constitution to allow himself another term in office.

Perón's presidency took another tragic hit shortly after his reelection in 1952. Eva, the country's wildly popular first lady, died from cancer at just thirty-three years old. She had been beloved by the people, and there was a massive outpouring of national grief at her death. She had never held office as a political leader, but shortly before she died, the Congress of Argentina officially titled her "Spiritual Leader of the Nation."

But even had she lived, her support, political shrewdness, and popularity could not have pulled her husband from the downward spiral in which he had become caught. The military was losing patience with him. The people were losing patience with him. And after 1953, when a group of Peronists took control of parochial schools and legalized divorce, the Catholic Church was losing patience with him. Anti-church demonstrations in Buenos Aires led to him and his cabinet being excommunicated by the Vatican itself.

Perón's final days in office were a quick descent into turmoil. Labor strikes again paralyzed the country. One hundred thousand protesting middle-class workers blanketed the streets of Buenos Aires. Days later, a counterdemonstration was organized by thousands of

Peronist workers. Dozens of military officers rose up in mutiny, and warplanes bombed Peronist protesters in the streets, killing 156 and injuring hundreds more.

But it was being on the outs with the Catholic Church that was the final nail in Perón's coffin. It was just the excuse the military needed to oust him from office. General Eduardo Lonardi launched the Revolución Libertadora ("Liberating Revolution") in September of 1955. Perón faced an ultimatum from the military: resign or civil war would ensue. Perón resigned, choosing exile over potential civil violence. Though he disappeared from Argentina, Peronism would not.

Chapter 20 – The Return of Perón

Successive changes in political leaders and regimes marked the following years. Government violence against its own people swelled in the number of instances and escalated in their horrific nature. The cost of living became untenable.

Perón, who was exiled in Spain, kept his finger on the pulse of what was happening in his home country. Peronists had split into factions and now fought each other. He sent his new wife, Isabel, back to Argentina in an attempt to mediate between the factions. Their efforts came to nothing when President Arturo Illia was removed from office.

Radical presidencies gave way to military regimes. Kidnappings became rampant and included high-profile people like ex-president Pedro Eugenio Aramburu. Torture, assassinations, and executions were carried out by radical groups. Aramburu was among those executed for ordering Peronist executions during his presidency.

In 1971, President Alejandro Lanusse faced a floundering economy and national discord. Drastic measures needed to be taken, and he decided on a huge gamble—letting "the old man" Perón return to Argentina's political arena. But getting Perón back into the country would take time—time they didn't have. In the March 1973 elections, it was decided that Peronist leader Héctor Cámpora would stand in for Perón as president of the country. But in the minds of the people, he was no substitution for Perón.

Political violence continued escalating. High-ranking military officials became targets of guerilla militants. The country was again near the brink of civil war. Many felt that only Perón's return could quell the chaos.

Perón, seventy-seven years old and in poor health, returned to Argentina several months after the election and was installed in office. However, his third time as the country's president would be short-lived. Before he died in office in July 1974, he managed to do something he was unable to do in his previous terms as president— have his wife positioned as his vice president. But Isabel, a former Panamanian troupe dancer, was not equipped to deal with the immense challenges the country faced.

Before Perón died, the country's economic woes again reared their ugly head. The inexperienced Isabel, now saddled with these problems after her husband's death, could not bring things under control.[46] Labor unrest and violence continued; inflation soared, and unemployment numbers grew.

Though she did not have the same charisma or held the adoration of the people like Eva did, the country still threw their support behind her, at least at first. She installed new cabinet members and made a few economic policies that were met with approval, even by leftist party members. She tried to solve the foreign debt problem by printing more money. However, her failure to meet with constituents and political groups left a sour taste, and any leeway she had been granted due to sympathy over her husband's death quickly dried up.

---

[46] As vice president when Perón died, Isabel stepped into the presidency as his successor. She became the first female president in the Western Hemisphere.

Under her short presidency, the country experienced more tumult. If Argentinians had thought the economy was bad before Perón returned from Spain, it was nearly incomprehensible under Isabel, as inflation rose by 400 percent. Her obvious Peronist leanings helped continue the bloodshed between radicals and conservatives. Many innocent bystanders came to be among the numbers killed. Isabel was on the thinnest of ice. Her campaign to unseat leftist university employees and governors, along with a spate of political murders, further weakened her standing. The economy was imploding as violence was exploding.

More problems emerged. José López Rega, the country's minister of social welfare, was quickly becoming a liability. He exhibited strange behavior in public (such as silently mouthing Isabel's words as she was speaking them) and was embroiled in other scandals. He was known to have fascist sympathies and had business relationships with high-profile fascists like Italian Licio Gelli. His newly formed organization, the paramilitary Argentine Anticommunist Alliance, was a thinly veiled death squad, carrying out kidnappings and as many as three hundred murders between 1973 and 1974. Among those targeted were professors, activists, and other prominent public figures. The Argentine public became increasingly disenchanted.

The country was now again on the brink of anarchy. The situation was further aggravated when, in November 1974, Isabel declared a state of siege, essentially stripping citizens of all civil liberties. However, it did nothing to slow the terrorist conflicts. The military became increasingly anxious to get her out of office. Politically moderate officers, wanting to try a peaceful and willing ousting, urged her to resign. She stubbornly refused, declaring her intention to finish her term, which didn't end until May 1977.

Knowing that her grip on power was hanging by a thread, she scrambled to find a solution that didn't involve her resignation. As a compromise, she made an offer to hold new elections before her term ended, but it was too little, too late. More forceful action was decided by the military.

A bloodless coup was staged on March 24th, 1976, when General Jorge Rafael Videla (who had previously urged her resignation) seized power and put Isabel under house arrest. She would remain in custody until her trial in 1981. She was convicted and allowed to live in exile in Spain.[47]

Though what they called "the coup to end all coups" ended the Perón era, it would not end the turmoil and violence within the country.

---

[47] In 1983, Isabel Perón was pardoned by the Argentine government and allowed to leave Spain.

Chapter 21 – The "Dirty War" and the Falkland War

Under the regime of General Videla, the Argentine military began what came to be known as the "Dirty War." Excessive measures by the military abounded. True subversives, those just sympathetic to left-wing ideologies, and truly innocent bystanders were all swept up in the vicious campaign to wipe out right-wing enemies.

Organized revolutionaries bent on ousting the general and installing a socialist regime funded their war chest through kidnappings and robberies. Videla began an all-out war against the revolutionaries. The public supported action against the rebels, hoping that the military could restore and reorder their fractured society. The revolutionaries, for their part, did not fear war, but Videla instituted a strategy he was sure they would fear.

The number of those who "disappeared" mounted frighteningly. They were rarely seen or heard from again. Using disappearances as a scare tactic, Videla strategically created an atmosphere of terror.

Arrests and abductions were performed by "off-duty" military figures. Torture and executions (with some people horrifically being thrown into the ocean from military planes) became rampant—as many as twenty thousand were caught in Videla's campaign.

The cost of winning the conflict was extremely high. Aside from the thousands of deaths, the Dirty War had made Argentina a pariah on the world scene. Foreign relations would continue to be strained when the decision was made to revisit a previous attempt at recapturing the British-held Falkland Islands.

War for the Falkland Islands

When General Leopoldo Galtieri took the reins from Videla in 1983, he was looking for a way to redeem the regime in the eyes of the people. He would finish the plan started during World War II and reclaim the Falkland Islands for Argentina. The move generated a burst of patriotism and enthusiasm. The people had no idea how disastrous a maneuver they were applauding.

The Argentine people mistakenly believed that Britain would not care about the small islands they had seized thousands of miles from their own shores. In the minds of the Argentine military, the desolate islands, with their mere 1,800 inhabitants, would not be worth a war effort, especially in such an isolated location. But if the British did resist, Argentina was banking on the United States backing them up. Their assumptions were way off base.

On April 2nd, 1982, the military launched a quick offensive on the small garrison located on the islands and was able to swiftly take it over. The British response was quick and forceful. A British submarine sank an Argentine ship (killing 360), and the superior British forces quickly overtook the Argentine military on land. The Argentines put up a good fight, but the British were too strong. The war ended on June 14th.

Patriotism and support for the war quickly died after the rapid collapse of the Argentine forces on the islands. The people turned to demonstrations against Galtieri, who not only faced criticism from the public for the debacle but also from within his own government. He resigned in disgrace.

His successor, Reynaldo Bignone, gave hope to the people after this, promising a return to civilian government. It would pave the way for Argentina's transition back to democracy.

Conclusion

In the early 2000s, Argentina still faltered under an economic crisis, plagued by inflation and foreign debt. The government's handling of the economy angered Argentinians, who violently protested in demonstration of their dissatisfaction.

However, in 2004, recovery from the crisis was underway. The country, like all others, still experiences its challenges. Buenos Aires faces particular challenges within its urban landscape. But despite the violence, crises, and problems it has faced over the past centuries, there are hopeful signs for the country. Its economy continues to recover and burgeon, helped along by its technological development and an increase in globalization. Internet cafés that popped up in the 1990s helped connect Argentinians with each other and the rest of the world, leading to social improvements.

Remnants of native cultures have left shadows of influences that have carried into modern times. The country's colorful culture has been shaped through the past by many different types of people from all over the world, as they brought their traditions with them as they made their home in Argentina.

The country's identity is also reflected in stories and songs of gauchos and other heroes. Their epic traditional lifestyle might be part of a bygone era, but some still remain, working as ranch hands. Saddle up to a bar in cattle country, and you might just come face to face with one of these famed cowboys of legend.

Buenos Aires, to this day, is the epicenter of the country's modern culture, helping to shape the country through education, arts, radio, and other media.

Patagonia and Tierra del Fuego retain their desolate beauty, the pampas still stretch to the horizon, and the Andes Mountains continue to tower, creating an alluring place for visitors and citizens alike.

Here's another book by Captivating History that you might like

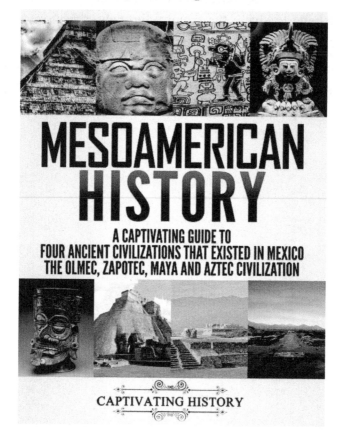

Free Bonus from Captivating History (Available for a Limited time)

Hi History Lovers!

Now you have a chance to join our exclusive history list so you can get your first history ebook for free as well as discounts and a potential to get more history books for free! Simply visit the link below to join.

Captivatinghistory.com/ebook

Also, make sure to follow us on Facebook, Twitter and Youtube by searching for Captivating History.

References

Todd L. Edwards. 2008. *Argentina: A Global Studies Handbook.* Santa Barbara, Calif.: ABC-CLIO https://archive.org/details/argentinaglobals0000edwa/page/56/mode/2 up?q=martin+fierro

José M.F. Pastor José Bonilla David J. Keeling. *History of Buenos Aires.* https://www.britannica.com/place/Buenos-Aires/History

Lieutenant Musters. 1872. *On the Races of Patagonia.* Source: The Journal of the Anthropological Institute of Great Britain and Ireland, 1872, Vol. 1 (1872) Published by: Royal Anthropological Institute of Great Britain and Ireland https://www.jstor.org/stable/2840953

Richard A. Crooker. 2004. *Argentina.* Philadelphia: Chelsea House Publishers https://archive.org/details/argentina0000croo/page/56/mode/2up

Huw Hennessy. 1999. *Insight Guide Argentina.* Langenscheidt Publishing Group https://books.google.com/books?id=WNOm_mfkxmYC&pg=PA33#v =onepage&q&f=false

"Argentina History." https://www.whatargentina.com/argentina-history.html

"Southern South America: Southeastern Argentina | Ecoregions | WWF." World Wildlife Fund.

Cayuqueo, Pedro (2020). *Historia secreta mapuche 2*. Santiago de Chile: Catalonia. pp. 34–37. ISBN 978-956-324-783-1.

Robert Silverberg. *Reflections: The Strange Case of the Patagonian Giants.*

http://www.asimovs.com/assets/1/6/Reflections_StrangeCase-Dec11.pdf

José Imbolloni, "De Historia Primitiva de América. Los grupos raciales aborígenes." Madrid, Cuadernos de Historia Primitiva Año II, 1957

Britannica, The Editors of Encyclopedia. "Guaraní." Encyclopedia Britannica, https://www.britannica.com/topic/Guarani. Accessed 7 July 2021.

"Juan and Evita Peron." https://www.whatargentina.com/juan-peron.html

Helen Dwyer, "History of Argentina – Ancient to Modern." https://www.chimuadventures.com/blog/2016/11/history-of-argentina/

Contenidos Patagona. "The Selk'nam (Onas) and the Yamanas." https://www.newworldencyclopedia.org/entry/Argentina#cite_note-2

"History Of Patagonia." https://www.patagonia-argentina.com/en/selknam-onas-yamanas/

Philip McCouat. "Art and Survival in Patagonia: How destroyed Patagonian Indian cultures live on through their art." http://www.artinsociety.com/art-and-survival-in-patagonia.html

Mitch Williamson. *The Incan military – Military Organization: Weapons and Warfare* History and Hardware of Warfare https://weaponsandwarfare.com/2015/12/28/the-incan-military-military-organization/

Handbook of South American Archaeology edited by Helaine Silverman, William Isbel Springer Science & Business Media, Apr 6, 2008 - *Social Science* - 1192 pages

"Biography of Juan Díaz de Solís (1470-1516)."
https://thebiography.us/en/diaz-de-solis-juan

Carl Waldman, Jon Cunningham, Encyclopedia of Exploration. *City of the Caesars.* New York 2004, ISBN 0-8160-4676-X Compiled by World Heritage Encyclopedia https://www.heritage-history.com/site/hclass/british_middle_ages/ebooks/pdf/ober_cabot.pdf

"Pedro de Mendoza." Encyclopedia Britannica. 2008. Encyclopedia Britannica Online. 08 Oct. 2008.

John A. Crow. "Conquest of the River Plate." *The Epic of Latin America.* 4th ed. New York: University of California P, 1992. 129-30

Frederick A. Ober. 1908. *John and Sebastian Cabot, Heroes of American History.* Harper & Brothers Publishers, New York & London

Enrique Udaondo, *Diccionario biográfico colonial argentino* (1945), pp. 357-365. https://www.encyclopedia.com/humanities/encyclopedias-almanacs-transcripts-and-maps/garay-juan-de-1528-1583

David J. Keeling. "History of Buenos Aires."
https://www.britannica.com/place/Buenos-Aires/History

Adventures and Misadventures of Don Juan de Garay, Second Founder of Buenos Aires. www.elhistoriador.com.ar/aventuras-y-desventuras-de-don-juan-de-garay-segundo-fundador-de-buenos-aires/

Justo, Liborio. 1968. *Our Vassal Homeland: History of Argentine Colonialism.* Schapire, Buenos Aires.

Buenos Aires Foundation Minutes. Digest ordinances, regulations, agreements, decrees, etc. of the municipality of Buenos Aires, Buenos Aires, Editorial de la Universidad, 1890, p. 7.

Andres M. Carretero. *The Argentine Gaucho: Past and Present.* Buenos Aires, Editorial Sudamericana, p. 138.

Pueblos Originarios. "Jeronimo Luis de Cabrera."
https://pueblosoriginarios.com/biografias/cabrera_jeronimo.html

"The streets of Salta and their names." *El Intransigente*, December 29, 2008.
https://web.archive.org/web/20140201184247/http://www.elintransige
nte.com/notas/2008/12/29/salta-9910.asp

Gonzalo de Abreu and the Justice of Cabrera. Archived February 1, 2014 at the Wayback
Machine https://web.archive.org/web/20070928163836/http:/www.end
epa.org.ar/JUNTO%20A%20LOS%20PUEBLOS%20INDIGENAS
%20II%20ANEXO.doc

Ana Diaz Biographical Dictionary of Argentine Women. Lily Sosa de Newton. Plus Ultra.

Isabel Hernandez. 1995. *Los indios de Argentina (in Spanish)*. Abya Yala. pp. 145–146.

"Pedro Bohoroquez." https://www.elhistoriador.com.ar/pedro-bohorquez/

Tres Guerras, Equipo Nacional de Pastoral Aborigen (ENDEPA). https://web.archive.org/web/20070928163836/http:/www.endepa.org.a r/JUNTO%20A%20LOS%20PUEBLOS%20INDIGENAS%20II%2 0ANEXO.doc

"Las ruinas de los Quilmes, una historia de heroísmo y destierro." https://web.archive.org/web/20070928163836/http:/www.endepa.org.a r/JUNTO%20A%20LOS%20PUEBLOS%20INDIGENAS%20II%2 0ANEXO.doc

Dr. Miguel Ángel De Marco Invasion, Reconquest, Defense of Buenos Aires 1806-1807.

http://uca.edu.ar/es/pabellon-de-bellas-artes/muestras/muestras-2007/invasion--reconquista--defensa-de-buenos-aires-1806-1807

Ministry of Defense Argentina. "On July 5, 1807 began the iron defense of the city of Buenos Aires."

https://www.argentina.gob.ar/noticias/el-5-de-julio-de-1807-comenzaba-la-ferrea-defensa-de-la-ciudad-de-buenos-aires

Reseña sobre la historia de Neuquén. Archived 2006-05-01 at the Wayback Machine

Dana Ward. "Timeline of Anarchism in Argentina." Anarchy Archives. Pitzer College. http://dwardmac.pitzer.edu/Anarchist_Archives/worldwidemovements/argtimeline.html

"Chronology: Argentina's Turbulent History of Economic Crises." Reuters Staff. https://www.reuters.com/article/us-argentina-debt-chronology/chronology-argentinas-turbulent-history-of-economic-crises-idUSKBN0FZ23N20140730

R. Spruk. *The Rise and Fall of Argentina.* Lat Am Econ Rev 28, 16 (2019). https://latinaer.springeropen.com/articles/10.1186/s40503-019-0076-2

Merco Press. "Falklands: The Argentine Military Planned Invasion during World War II." https://en.mercopress.com/2013/11/14/falklands-the-argentine-military-planned-invasion-during-world-war-ii

"Argentina in World War II." https://www.globalsecurity.org/military/world/argentina/history-ww2.htm

"High-ranking Nazi Official Adolf Eichmann Captured." https://www.history.com/this-day-in-history/eichmann-captured